Jen

Thank you for supporting m

Love a Blessing

Barbara Ridgway /d.t. Higgins

2020

Into the Shadow

Diary of an African-American Female Correctional Officer

Barbara Ridgeway

Copyright 2019 Barbara Ridgeway
All rights reserved

FIRST EDITION

All Scripture quotes from King James Version, The Original African Heritage Study Bible, Third Printing, copyright 1993, The Jameis Winston Publishing Company.
Reference *And Still I Rise* author Maya Angelou third volume of property published Random House in 1971
I, Tina autobiography by Tina Turner, Published by William Morrow and Company in 1986. Reference Department of Justice webpage, Bureau of Prisons Policies Rules and Regulations

TABLE OF CONTENTS

Dedication to Parents		ix
Memory of Lt. Cole		xi
Acknowledgements: My Village		xiii
Preface		1
Introduction		3
Chapter 1	Kentucky State Maximum Security Penitentiary	5
Chapter 2	Federal Bureau of Prison-Department of Justice	13
Chapter 3	Federal Detention Center (FDC), Oakdale, LA	36
Chapter 4	FCI, Memphis, TN	49
Chapter 5	FCI, Tallahassee, FL	73
Chapter 6	Federal Correctional Complex, Butner, NC	88
Chapter 7	Inmate/Staff Manipulation	98
Chapter 8	Affirmative Action and Harassment in the Highest Level	104
Chapter 9	The Dangers for a Female Correctional Officer	109
Chapter 10	The Dangers of Inmate Escort Trips	113
Chapter 11	The Oath	119
Chapter 12	Summary	121
Appendix		127
About the Author		141

Dedication

My Parents: Nell & Sylvester Ridgeway

Giving all honor and glory to God who held my steps to His path; my feet have not stumbled. Psalm 17:5. My parents raised me to be all I could be. They raised me to have great moral values. To treat others how you want to be treated if not better. To always lead and never follow. Who loved me with a strong hand but gave me wings to fly and fly I did. Thanks Mom and Dad for all you did and more. Your love shines in me every day.

In Memory of

D. Richard F. "Dick" Cole

August 19, 1943 - April 15, 2019

Lt. Cole, you saw things in me I didn't know I had. You believed in me more than I believed in myself. I couldn't have been the Lieutenant I was had it not been for you. Thank you for all you did for me and in me.

Acknowledgements

My Village

"And whatever you do, whether in word or deed, do it all in the name of the Lord Jesus, giving thanks to God the Father through Him."
Colossians 3:17

- **Angela Martin,** my daughter whom I love dearly, my number one cheerleader. She has encouraged me, supported me, and refused to allow me to give up. She saw the vision.
- **Cameron, Chris, and Jacob,** my three heartbeats, you guys have always supported and encouraged me throughout your little short lived lives. I am because of you guys. Nannee love you guys to the moon and back.
- **My family, "The Ridgeways,"** thank you for always being there for me through this journey. I know it was your prayers and added support that got me through. When I missed family functions, holiday gatherings, and there was a lot of them, especially Thanksgiving, you made sure I had pictures, phone calls and mostly you made sure Angela was taken care of. Words can't express the love and appreciation I have for each and everyone of you.
- I am so grateful that **FCI, Lexington, Kentucky** was my first duty station. Everything I learned and knew in Lexington prepared me for every situation I encountered. Without hesitation I was able to stand my ground and stand firm. I believed in myself because they

believed in me. There is nothing better than the Lexington connection; it touches me no matter where I am.
- **Captain Bezy,** who promoted me to GS-9 in house Lieutenant at Lexington. You stayed in the fight for my promotion and refused to give up or allow me to give up. I can never thank you enough for your support.
- **Warden Hambrick,** who taught me how to balance between doing it to you and doing it for you. I became a people person under your watch.
- **Mr. Matthews, Southeast Regional Director,** thank you for always answering my phone calls and connecting me to the right people to get me to the next step in my career.
- **Mr. Greer,** who always picked up the phone and made it happen without question.
- **Warden Beeler,** you planted the seed when you hired me. I started my career with you and ended it with you, who can say. You gave me room to grow and even to this day have never let me down. You followed my career and life for 20 plus years. I will forever be grateful to you.
- **Lt. Duron,** I can't say enough about you. You adopted me as your Bureau child and raised me up right. There was no lesson that you didn't teach me.
- **Warden Holder,** you were friend, my confidant and advisor. You made sure that everyone you knew, I knew. That everyone had my name to go with my face. That all phone numbers were correct. You made me a member of your Bureau family. I could never thank you enough or begin to pay you back for all you did for me in the Bureau, and you did a lot.
- **Captain Hudson,** who gave me wind and allowed me to soar.
- **Warden Clark,** my first female Warden, who showed me how to be myself, do my job and look good doing it. I still have love for you and truly appreciate all your support
- **Warden Guzik,** you took a chance on me as a rookie GS-11 Lieutenant and allowed me the room to grow in my career. Thank you for believing in me, supporting me and trusting me enough to work for you not once, but twice.

Acknowledgements

- **Sylvia Ahrens,** an award-winning author, my writing mentor who became the #001 convict. I could not have achieved my dream had it not been for your encouragement. She is armed with an amazing heart and mind, dangerous because we think alike. Thank you Sylvia for all your patience, time and energy.
- **"Power to Exhale,"** an amazing group of women who have encouraged me to "jump" and God will provide the net. Whatever your dreams are to go get them. Thank you women of "Power to Exhale" for your support to lay my fear of failure down on the altar. powertoexhale.org

Preface

I've been on this with my mother my entire life. Have often stated that my house was "FCI (Federal Correctional Institution) Higgins" because of her strict rules, but I managed to survive. People fail to realize the sacrifices that correctional officers make, missing family functions, failed relationships and marriages, to isolation. Police officers arrest the bad guys and courts sentence the bad guys but both of these entities pretty much are done at this point. But correctional officers continue to be locked up with guys sometimes up to sixteen hours a day. The police and the courts get the glory for taking them off the streets, but the real unsung heroes go unnoticed and unappreciated. We deal with violence, manipulation, mental and physical exhaustion, and harassment on a daily basis. No one ever takes the time to say "thank you" for keeping society safe.

Many of the correctional officers, such as my mom, really love what they did and wouldn't have chosen another career, if they had to do it all over again. I have watched my mother work her way from the Maximum Security Prison in Eddyville, Kentucky, to being the first and only African American female Lieutenant in Federal Institutions. She didn't realize it at the time she was history in the making. She accomplished these accomplishments in true "Barbara Fashion," while remaining "true diva and lady she is." I am so proud of her and all she has accomplished. She is truly the best friend, sister, aunt, nannee, and mom anyone could ask for.

        Love your daughter,
        Angela

Introduction

When God first gave me this idea to write my story I had no idea that this was the direction in which I would be going. I was truly out of my element, so I just allowed Him to order my steps. I know He said write your vision down on the tablet, Habakkuk 2:2, but this was way too big and scary for me to envision, let alone write. But we all know nothing is too big for God. And He said, "Do not be anxious." Philippians 4:6.

I've worked for both Federal and State Correctional Institutions a total of 29 years, and I am so proud to be a part of such an elite group of men and women. This book is about my goals and aspirations; therefore, I choose not to talk about the haters because every transfer or promotion was preselected due to my hard work and God's grace. This career is not for the weak or faint of heart. You either run with the big dogs or stay on the porch. I chose to get off the porch and run with the big dogs. There were times when my big girl panties were not big enough; that was when I had to pull my pants up and feel my imaginary balls, no joke. There are no secrets revealed about the state or federal prison systems. These pages are filled with my journey and final destination in a male-dominant field.

The day the magic happened, I was coming across Central Park at the Federal Correctional Institution (FCI) in Lexington and saw all the white shirts standing on the front steps. I knew that was what I wanted to be. So my journey began, but it took a village.

I'm still impressed by what I saw that day. I made many sacrifices along the way. I would receive a phone call from the Captain while I was on vacation asking if I could cut my vacation short one or two days early because he needed me to come back to the institution. I would be home watching television when the phone would ring and off to work I would go, no matter the time or the hour.

The thing I never gave up was my integrity, how to treat people, and the values that my parents instilled in me. I never forgot where I came from. I never stood on anyone's back to get ahead. I did my best to help anyone along the way. To teach them the best way I knew how, to be an open book. I got mine on my feet and not in the sheets.

My personal life was nonexistent. As bad as it might sound, I loved every phone call because in order to reach my goals, I needed to come out of the shadows.

Chapter 1

Kentucky State Maximum Security Penitentiary

As I start the last and final chapters in my life, I begin to look back at all the ups and downs that my God brought me through. I achieved full retirement for the first time ever in my life. My prayers are that God continues to order my steps.

My true working experience started in 1977 at the early age of 25, when I stepped inside of the Kentucky State Penitentiary, also known as the "Castle on the Cumberland," located in Eddyville, Kentucky, on Lake Barkley on the Cumberland River. I was an African American female Correctional Officer in an all-male maximum security institution or prison. It was a horrible place to work even today, especially being a female, but being a single mom I had to do what I needed to do.

But like most jobs you come to work, do your job, and go home. My prayers were to make it home safe. I felt that females were terribly disrespected at the time, but affirmative action was alive and well in those days. Quotas had to be made. I was told that I was part of that quota and that the numbers only counted during the hiring process and not in the firing process. Being told that I would not make it through training just gave me fuel. The worst thing you can ever tell me is "you can't" or "you won't." And guess what, I made it through the training with high marks, but it didn't change the fact that I was female in a male-dominant field. Working there was hard because of both inmates and male staff. It made me hard and tough. Working there was not for the weak; inmates as well as the male staff would eat you alive and spit you back out. My plan was to complete the six-week training and quit, but at the time the money was too good to quit so I stayed.

It was a very scary and frightening place to work whether you are male or female. It housed the baddest of the bad inmates: first degree murderers, raptists, death row inmates, and inmates with violent and disruptive behavior from other Kentucky prisons. When you were sent to Eddyville, that was it, you couldn't get any farther down. The inmates would welcome a body bag. It is where the executions of Kentucky death inmates are conducted. Hell, during the orientation process they even showed us the electric chair!

I was definitely in over my head. I had no earthly idea what I was doing, but I came to work every day, a forty-five minute drive to and from home. The biggest thing that helped me as I was learning my way through was a lot of the guys in lockup were from my hometown and knew my family or my brothers. So, they helped me out. The Ridgeway name was well known and respected in my hometown.

Chapter 1

One of the biggest challenges was keeping inmates out of my face. As soon as I got one inmate out of my face, another one would appear and make it difficult to control the area I was assigned to. These guys are very good at watching officers and getting their patterns down. So I started watching them and their movements while making sure I stayed in the open spaces. I got good at it too. Now I was an evil black bitch who would never get a man.

Visitors will always try to sneak something by the officers. One time while I was working the visitation area, my sister's boyfriend came to visit his brother who was locked up. While I was processing him in to visit, he asked me if he could wear his watch in. I told him yes but to make sure to wear it back out. We already knew that he had planned on giving the watch to his brother while he was visiting. When the sign states or someone says that all calls are monitored, please believe it. Phone surveillance revealed to us about the watch and that his brother was planning to bring it in. As I was escorting him out, I asked him about the watch. He snapped his fingers and stated that he forgot it. I had tried to warn him when I told him to make sure he wore it out. His brother was being held in the inmates' search room with the watch on his wrist waiting for the confirmation call. Needless to say, my sisters' boyfriend went to jail for introduction of contraband into a correctional facility and his brother went to lockup on something that he could have and should have mailed in. I called my sister and told her how her boyfriend tried it on me. She was furious that he tried to take advantage of me and put me in that position. Once he was released from jail, he cried straight to her that

I should have given him a pass on bringing the watch in. Can you say goodbye to that relationship? I liked him too. I wasn't going to lose my job and my integrity over his dumb ass.

Inmates would use anyone or any means necessary to get what they wanted into the institution. I simply hated to work the visiting room because of all the ways the visitors attempted to bring contraband into the prison. You just read one example about the watch, that was just the tip of the iceberg and women are the worst. During that time we didn't have walk through metal detector, only hand held scanners. These women would use their babies, I have found drugs inside of the baby's diaper, while moving the babies' milk bottle up and down I noticed a plastic bag inside of the baby bottle, of course it was drugs. The diaper bag was just a way to bring all kinds of contraband into the institution, we had to stop allowing them in the institution. I would find anything from pills to marijuana cigarettes sewed into the seams of clothing. The first time I found out about a false button Pepsi can was on visits. There was always a County Sheriff standing in visiting processing area, as I was searching a visitor picnic basket, I pulled out a Pepsi can, the Sheriff walked over to me and asked me for the can. He began to point out all the marks and scratches on the top around the lid of the can. He then opened the can and pulled out the contents of drugs. I was dumbfounded, it would be my first but not the last time seeing this, but then I became angry because no telling how many soda cans I let into the visiting area, so the drugs would reach the yard. The visiting area keeps you busy and on your toes. Everything back then was done by hand, so it

Chapter 1

wasn't easy to find or catch the person(s) bringing it in.

The special housing unit (SHU) was four floors at the time, a two-sided cell house that housed protective custody inmates, maximum custody inmates, and death row inmates all on separate ranges or floors, with well over a hundred inmates at the time. Inside the unit was a steel cage manned by two people who worked the cage or control center for the SHU. Each officer worked two levels of the unit, controlling the inmates' cell doors, passing out equipment to the range officers like restraints and mace, supplying personal items to the inmates, and anything else that was needed for the running of the unit. There were a total of eight ranges with one officer per range.

Due to the fights and assaults, all inmates were restrained with handcuffs and legirons when out of their cells, which included their one hour of recreation. I worked the upper two levels. Whenever there was an emergency, and there were plenty of them, I would report to wherever the emergency was and order inmates to go in their cells. Another officer would pass out emergency equipment in order for the officers to enter the range to get control of the situation.

There was this one time during a very cold winter when the inmates refused to go back in their cells. They broke out the range windows on the unit, trashed the range, flooded the cells, and refused all orders to return to their cells. Gas or mace was not an option because they had broken out the windows. The Captain of the unit decided to use the fire hoses. He sprayed the range with water until the inmates were happy to go in their cells. It was the coldest day I ever spent on any job. They laid in those wet beds on that cold range for days. That was my first incident, but I can assure you it was not my last. It was just the beginning.

I had a little friend in SHU who was a special needs inmate and had been locked up for years. He called me Barbara. No matter what I said or how many times I tried to correct him, he continued to call me by my first name. Pick your battles. He just wanted someone to talk to him. He was on the same tier or level that I was. When I was not busy or I had some downtime, I would talk to him since his cell was close to the cage. One day he took his eye out and put it in his hand and said, "Hey, Barbara, I see you." At first it scared the hell out of me, and I then realized that he had a prosthetic eye. We both cracked up laughing.

One inmate on the same range that my special needs friend was on, stuck his penis through the bars at me. I tried to catch it in the cell door but missed. When my little friend heard him laughing and making a comment about it, he said, "Don't worry, Barbara. I'm going to get him." I thanked him and dismissed what he said because he was recreation and housed alone. A couple of days had passed and the guy was still flashing himself. I was over it by then, but he was still laughing and thinking he was doing something big and bold. It was my friend's day for recreation, but he didn't say a word. The next thing I knew I heard someone screaming like they were dying or in a horror movie. Everybody working in the cellhouse came running to my range. My friend came running back to his cell like he was trying out for the Olympic games and said, "Barbara, he won't

Chapter 1

mess with you again." When the officers reached the range and went in to check to see what that happened, one of the officers said that my little friend had thrown hot baby oil on that dude. When he tried to wipe it off, his skin came off with it. He really messed him up. That was a warning to the entire range not to mess with or disrespect Barbara. I don't know where that dude went, but he was escorted to medical because he damn sure needed some skin donated. He was not put back on that range. My little friend didn't play with his ass; he dropped the mike on his ass. After that nobody tested him or me again. However, he continued to give the officers hell, flooding his cell, and the only time he would stop was when I said that it affected me or my work area.

I remember one time an inmate had escaped; when I reported in for work that day, I was given a loaded shotgun and sent off into the woods as part of the search team. Keep in mind that this is country woods with a lot of tall trees and high weeds. As it was getting dark, the search was called off. At this time I had hooked up with a male officer when I saw movement out of the corner of my eye. That inmate was standing behind a tree, he was wearing green clothing standing there looking like the Incredible Hunk. I drew up my shotgun and pointed it at him. I don't know if I would have shot him, but I was looking like I would! The other officer with me fired his weapon and yelled that we found him. This was one of the scariest things to happen in my life. He really was a huge dude.

This still didn't give women any credibility or respect. I was married at the time, so when someone asked who had found the inmate and was told it was me, they commented, "Oh, not her husband?" The next day when I reported to work feeling really good and still high on adrenaline from finding the escapee, there was no "That a girl," no "You did a great job," no letter from the governor, no "Thank you" from the city, not even an employee of the month. It was back to work as usual. I was told that because I was a female in this type of environment it would be an embarrassment to the institution, that it would look bad. Years later I found out that I was the first and only female that had ever found an escaped inmate at that time!

Since I left the Kentucky State Penitentiary, they have added Supermax to the name. I still don't know why in the hell they called it "Castle on the Cumberland." It doesn't matter how pretty you make the outside, it is always the inside that counts. This is no different. Ugly is ugly.

Inmates were still assaulting staff and inmates, walking around with homemade shanks or weapons even though they are scanned with a handheld metal detector and pat searched constantly, whether they are on the yard or in their cell house or existing food service. There is disrespect for life, and it doesn't matter whose life it is. I had never witnessed such acts of violence in my life. White supremacist groups like skinheads and the KKK were the worst. That type of hatred is pure evil.

Eight and a half years later, with little to no respect toward females, it was time to go.

Chapter 2

Federal Bureau of Prison-Department of Justice
FMC, Lexington, KY

In November of 1985, I interviewed for a Correctional Officer position for the Department of Justice. I had to go in front of an interview board. I was a wreck waiting to happen. This interview panel is all you would think it would be: Stone faces, hard glances/looks, no smiling, total intimidation. It was working, but I managed to pull it all together and did very well. I was so proud of myself. I made a very good impression with the interview panel.

Once the interview was over, I was sent out to wait in the Human Resource Office. I was very excited because I knew I was in, a Federal Correctional Officer, doing all the paperwork for my new position. After sitting there for so long, however, I began to have doubts and began to become very unsure of myself. Just then one of the interviewers came out and apologized for taking so long. My test score was unusually high so they called the testing office to inquire about my high test scores.

What I thought was a set back God used as a set up. I was told that my test score was high because I had worked eight and a half years in an all-male maximum security prison. Ten points were automatically added to my test score, the same as if I was a veteran. The interviewer then looked at me and said to the Human Resource Officer, "If she doesn't get hired, I want to personally know why." My heart jumped out of my chest and started running and doing flip flops. To this day that man has been a pivotal part of my career and life.

Watch God... Worst background check ever according to the Federal Investigator.

I was a little black girl born and raised in Paducah, Kentucky, in an area called Acardica, where the entire neighborhood was related: aunties, uncles, grandparents and cousins. When I say it was a village, it was a village. Now, having said that, imagine if you will, two white guys dressed in black suits and ties asking questions about me. No one they questioned said they knew who I was, didn't know my parents or my brothers and sister. The investigators went from door to door and didn't receive one bit of information about me or my family. They actually talked to my mother and wasn't sure if it was her. Even the corner grocery store didn't give them any information, a store that had been there all my young life and knew us by our names. The "chief" of the village was my mother. Nothing was said or told until she and only she gave the ok.

At some point the Investigators informed me that the background check on me was stalled because no one would talk to them or answer any questions about me. They further stated that I didn't even exist. It was the worst background check that they had ever done, but that they were instructed to get it done because the Bureau wanted to keep me.

> "And we know that all things work together for good to them that love God, to those who are called according to His purpose."
> **Romans 8:28**

At this point I had to call the "chief" and inform her that if no one talked to the investigators I would not get hired. The gates to the village finally opened! Needless to say I was hired but even then I was on a bumpy road. Switching from State to Federal was not an easy transition.

I had made it. I was hired by the Department of Justice, Bureau of Prisons. My first duty station was the Federal Correctional Institution (FCI) in Lexington, Kentucky. First of all, I came from an all-male maximum security institution where inmates were single celled and locked down, searched, screened for weapons on a daily basis. There was strict inmate accountability and manned gun towers. Inmates were escorted all day every day. Inmates were pat searched in and out of food service. I think you get the picture.

Now if you will, try and follow me and please keep up. I assure you that this is not a typo.

I was very excited to be working for The Bureau of Prisons, still new to the system and how things worked, but I was getting there. This was 1985. I was working the yard, still in training, and I saw men and women inmates walking around holding hands like they were on a date. Sitting on benches together, going to the prison movies, it was their own little world. My first thought was *What the What?* These women were dressed to the nines: stilettos, mink coats, hair and face immaculately done. Where in the world were they going? Did we just open the gates on the weekend so they could go out?

I soon learned it was called a co-correctional institution. Inmates were called walkies (because all they were supposed to do was walk around together). How was I supposed to adjust from maximum security to inmates walking around holding hands? It wasn't easy. What had I done? But like everything else in life that you want, you adjust and move on.

"I can do all things through Christ who strengthens me."
Philippians 4:13

Now it was time for me to go to correctional officers' training. Six weeks of intense training in Jesup, Georgia. I had never been out of Kentucky, and I had never been on a plane, and now I have to do both. Man! I had to repeat most of my training because I didn't have enough enthusiasm. During the hostage training, I was shot and killed because of my attitude. At this point, the training center was ready to send me back to my institution, but by the grace of God, I made it. Now it was time to get busy; after all, it was a journey just getting this far.

Rules and regulations had to be followed by both staff and inmates, and there seemed to be a lot of those to follow. Shifts were

Chapter 2

rotated every three months: three months of day watch, three months of evenings, and three of morning watch, which was the worst. Kiss weekends goodbye forever. At least, that's what it seemed like. At the state institution it was all day watch for me.

The probationary period was for one year. There were a lot of things that I was unable to do that I had done as a state officer on a daily basis. It was all daily routine for me and now I couldn't because I was a rookie (new officer). I became truly frustrated.

I was on the verge of quitting when a hard nosed, ole school Lieutenant noticed me and felt my frustration. He took me under his wings. Like everyone before him, he saw something in me that I didn't see in myself. He took me off of probation after six months because of my prior experience and gave me my wings to fly, and fly I did. Things were looking pretty good and the job was becoming much easier.

Then the challenges began. Not only was I transitioning from state to federal, but the institution was transitioning from a co-correctional institution to all-female institution. We had to pull all the men out because things were changing. The next change was we went to inmate uniforms (khakis pants and shirts). These women had to give up their diamonds, stilettos, mink coats, and wigs. All personal clothing had to go. It took months. We probably shook down every locker, every hole in the walls, and I'm sure we shook down the whole entire institution trying to find any piece of personal property we could.

During this time I was working on inmate property. This particular inmate had it all. She had two choices: she could mail it out or destroy her property. If she chose to mail it out, the institution would be responsible for the cost. Instead of mailing her property home, she chose to destroy it. That girl destroyed a long black sable mink coat. I had to tell myself, *Be strong. Don't let her see you cry.* (Smile.) Seriously though, most of these things were traded for a crack rock, so destroying it was not a problem.

After several long months of transitioning these women, we began to settle down and run the institution. Word came down that this wasn't working. We were removing all the women and returning the men. So here we were, back at it again. The only good thing about this transition was all institutions were now using inmate uniforms so there was no personal property to deal with.

That day I was reporting to work, I was coming through the sallyport (as you enter the inmate compound one door opens, while the other one stays closed). Right that's the door that slams behind you as you enter the inmate compound. As I crossed Central Park (yes, that was the name), the place where inmates could sit, talk and gather legally, I saw a group of White Shirts standing on the steps overlooking the park, just observing inmate activity. That was the greatest sight I'd ever seen. I knew that was what I wanted. They were all Lieutenants standing tall and strong, full of confidence.

"And The Lord answered me, and said, Write the vision, and make it plain upon the tablets. For the vision is yet for an appointed time, but at the end it shall speak, and not lie; though it tarry wait for it; because it will surely come, it will tarry."
Habakkuk 2:2-3

Chapter 2

From Job to Career

At some point my hard-nosed Lieutenant began pulling me to his shift. Now I was working the yard more, escorting inmates to and from SHU to medical appointments, visits, etc. He gave me more responsibility because of his faith and trust in me. When he asked me to do something and I wasn't sure if I could do it, he would say, "You can handle it." And of course I did. His response was, "I knew you could!" Not to say I didn't make a lot of mistakes, because I made a lot of them to the point that one mistake cost me a promotion. I needed that promotion for my next step up. But I kept on going and doing my thing. I know that all things work according to God's plan. Word on the yard from other officers was in order to get noticed you had to work the yard as Compound Officer. I was a rookie barely off probation, so the yard was out. All the Senior Officers were taking any and all positions that weren't a housing unit. No one wanted to work the housing unit and that's where I was. But not getting discouraged, I worked whatever housing unit I was put in. I tried to be the best Unit Officer I knew I could be, to the point that a certain Unit Manager would ask for me to be his Unit Officer every quarter. I made sure the unit was cleaned, floors were shining, bathroom clean and presentable. We never failed a unit inspection that had anything to do with me.

I made sure I conducted my inmate room searches and searched inmates and all bags coming in and out of the unit.

Then one day I made a huge bust inside of an inmate room. I

found needles and syringes taped to the back side of the heat radiator, marijiuana cigarettes taped to the button of his bed and several other items of contraband hidden in different areas of his room. I was thinking this was it, but the Unit Manager took the bust as his own. As it always does, the word got out that it was me and not the Unit Manager. I was down but I kept it moving because I had to get my white shirt.

All inmates' personal property needed to be mailed out or destroyed. Staff is not allowed to accept anything from an inmate.

Stepping out of the Shadows

Showing up early, staying late, completing paperwork, always being professional, responding to inmate emergencies, completing inmate searches, escorting inmates in and out of institution got me "Officer of the Quarter." I was happy, but it was not a promotion. However, it did give me the freedom to learn other areas of the institution to start the next level. I became Escort Officer, taking inmates to outside medical appointments. Dealing with the public on a daily basis while remaining professional was not an easy task but I did it.

So, yes in November, 1988 I went from GS-7 to GS-8 Officer! Yes! I make my first promotion. O Happy Day!

So now I was learning Lieutenant paperwork (because that was my next move) and training to be a Lieutenant. Teaching officers training classes, working in the Lieutenant Office and now the big one, Acting Lieutenant. This went on for about a year just doing whatever I was asked and making decisions on my own and dealing

Chapter 2

with inmate disciplinary problems. Correctional Officers were coming to me for assignments and inmate behavior problems. Life was good...

And then a new Captain arrived at the institution.

I needed to prove myself all over again. As I was still working as an Acting Lieutenant, it wasn't hard to do. I just kept doing my best and always going above and beyond my job. At some point, the new Captain approached me and stated that "he had been watching me and that I was doing my job." He started calling me Nancy Drew because I responded to all emergency situations with a camera. Then one day he approached me and stated that "he was going to have a GS-9 Lieutenant position opening soon and I should put in for it." What the what? Look at God! It was a long process.

> "God said it will surely come, it will tarry. Which means you're going to get it, but it's going to take awhile."
> **Habakkuk 2:2-3**

The GS-9 Lieutenants' position, would be an in-house promotion which meant I could stay in Lexington and continue to grow into my position. The longer it took for the announcement, the more impatient I became and doubts begin to set it. There were other officers who had more experience and have been there longer. There were officers who had ten years of experience applying for the same position and not having to move was the gravy. Being promoted to a Lieutenant and not having to move in those days was unheard of. This was the first time Lexington had done an in- house Lieutenant position in ten years. I was basically still a rookie. So, yes, my confidence level had dropped to the point that I started applying to other institutions. Imagine, if you will, every time I took an application for a GS-9 Lieutenant position for another location, instead signing it, that Captain ripped it up.

However, I did not realize that he was doing this for my own good and working toward God's purpose in my life. So, I finally calmed the hell down and began to trust the process.

I will never forget that day: I was an Acting Lieutenant. It was a Friday, I don't remember the date, but I do the day. As an Acting Lieutenant, I should have had an GS-11 Lieutenant with me at all times. That day it was just me. Anything that could go wrong, did. Inmates went out by ambulance, which mean roster adjustment to cover the inmate escort. There was a fight on the yard, more than the usual activity on the yard. I thought I handled everything pretty well. Right before shift ended, two GS-11 Lieutenants came into the office and asked me if anything unusual happened today.

They told me the Captain needed to see me. The Captain was Acting Assistant Warden at the time. So two Lieutenants literally escorted me out of the Lieutenant's Office across the compound at shift change. Officers were asking me, "What's going on?" I was told not to say anything. My mind was going crazy; I was a total mess.

When I reached the Assistant Warden's (AW) office, the Lieutenants left me sitting in the outer office for what seemed like hours. A few minutes later the Warden arrived and again I was escorted into the AWs office (remember my Captain was Acting AW). I was

Chapter 2

told to sit down, not asked but told. The Captain began to question me about my day," What had happened? Was there anything unusual that I didn't report?" I was feeling so intimidated, which usually doesn't happen to me, but I was at that moment . I thought I had done something wrong and could kiss my hard work and career goodbye. I had been proud of myself and thought I had done a pretty good job being by myself.

Just at my breaking point, the Warden said, "The reason you can't think of anything happening is because you didn't know. Congratulations, Lt. Higgins! You have just been promoted to GS-9 Lieutenant."

I praised God and jumped up and down. I took a moment to threaten my Captain and Lieutenants who were involved in this trick. Hallelujah!!! I was a total wreck. My nerves were shot, but by God's grace I had done it. In December 1989, I went from GS-8 Senior Officer to GS-9 Lieutenant (Jr. White Shirt). My next step was GS-11 Lieutenant. I was truly on my way.

"Do not be anxious about anything, but in every situation, by prayer and petition, with thanksgiving, present your request to God."
Philippians 6:6

Female inmates are a whole different breed when you compare them to male inmates.

Some officers think females are whiny, but I think male inmates whine just as much as the females. Males don't really snitch, females will snitch in your face. One time I was sitting in the Lieutenant's

Office when a female inmate came in and said, "Lt. Higgins there is a girl on the recreation yard with marijiauna in her leg cast." I sent a female officer out to the recreation yard to search the inmate. She reported back that she didn't find it. The inmate came back into the office again and said, "Lt. Higgins, you need to come out and get it, but I don't want her or the other inmates to know I told it, so when you bring her back to the office, bring me too." She had it all worked out. After making sure she was back on (her post) in the recreation yard, I approached the inmate with the cast on her leg and escorted both of them back to the Lieutenant's Office. Once in the office, I asked the inmate for the marijiauna and after a few surprising minutes and a short spurt of amnesia, she gave up the weed. Now keep in mind the inmate who told me wanted me to keep her name out of it. All of a sudden, this inmate jumped up and said, "Yea, bitch I told it. When your ass was out there puff, puff, pass, pass, and you wouldn't pass it to me. Now ain't nobody puffing." She was safe because she didn't pass it to her. The other one was escorted to SHU.

Had that been a male inmates, they would have fought right there in the office.

There was this special needs inmate who whipped everybody on the yard, but to her credit she was as big as she was crazy. During the four o'clock count we got a call for assistance in the Mental Health Unit. When I arrived on the unit this inmate was going off on the officer and walking up on him. She had her back to me, and she was so zoned out she didn't even know I was there. So I jumped on her back (did I say she was whipping everybody?) and we fell to the floor.

Chapter 2

I was still holding on to her when the other staff members arrived on the unit to assist. Hallelujah! It was not my day to get my ass whipped. As we were putting her in restraints, she turned her head to spit on me. It just missed me, but a tiny speck did get on the collar of my white shirt. Everyone in the room stopped what they were doing and all eyes were on me. I was told this (I don't remember) that I turned around in slow motion like the matrix and came back to the bed where the inmate was, but then I turned back around and walked out of the room. We laughed and joked about this forever, still do. Between me and you, I remembered that the video camera was on and running. God is good all the time.

The same inmate who was whipping everybody on the yard was now on SHU. The AW was making rounds in SHU. This man was one of those men who took the time to get dressed in the morning. He had a very nice expensve suit, tie and matching pocket handkerchief, and nice dry-cleaned shirt (you get the idea). You would have thought that Steve Harvey dressed him. She called the AW over to her cell door. We had given the AW several warnings not to put his head or face in the door grill, he was used to being the AW and having that false sense of authority. You guessed it! He put his face close to the door grill, and when he did, she went to the deepest part of her gut and spit in his face. I know her body had to be left dry because all her spit went into that man's face.

He was mad as hell, screaming and hollering to get her out of there. Where was he going to get her out of? She was already in SHU. She started laughing loudly at him. Did I mention that she didn't speak English? Not a drop! He was standing there with spit all over his face raising hell and she didn't even know what he was saying. The three of us stood there trying not to vomit, which would have made it worse for the AW. He should have been mad at himself; we told him not to do it. This was the same inmate who attempted to spit on me when I took her down from the Mental Health Unit. When the AW left that unit he was smoking hot; it's a good thing that he lived close to the institution. I bet the next time he'll listen to the officers. Needless to say, we laughed at that for days to come. On a serious tip, everyone was aware that spitting was what she did when she couldn't get her hands on you. Anytime we moved this inmate, we had to move her in a spit shield for staff protection.

This same inmate would smear vaseline all over her cell floor while she was housed in SHU, sit in her cell laughing at the top of her lungs, like we were going to come in her cell with all the vaseline on the floor. We were not allowed in her cell anyway unless we cuffed her up and took her out, so at the end of the day, the only one slipping and sliding on a slick floor was her. The funny part for me was watching her tiptoe around in that cell, so she wouldn't fall. Just like her, I was laughing as the top of my lungs. She was a real nut!

I just touched on the subject of *mental health inmates* which correctional officers had to deal with on a daily basis. It was nothing we took lightly. This woman was a very dangerous and volatile inmate, who injured several inmates and staff while I was there. To compound the dangers, she didn't speak any English. I'm sure her not speaking or understanding the language added to her frustration

Chapter 2

and behavior. Thank goodness we had a few staff who could translate Spainish. This was a very large inmate about the size of Fiona, Shrek's wife from the movie. Whether she was or was not on her medication didn't make a difference with the officers because she was always ready for a fight and not an easy take-down, whether it was inmates or staff. There was not much we did do with her because she had mental health status and sometimes just letting her huff and puff, as long as she was not hurting herself or someone else, if it will help her calm down. Some days it was not worth it because it took a village just to restrain her.

So, as usual, pick your battles.

Medication for mentally ill inmates was a whole different issue when they refused to take it. During my time there, the Psychologist could not force her or anyone to take medication without a court order. Laws change so I'm not sure what it is in today's time. When she or any other mental health inmate became too much for staff and the institution, they would need to petition the court or judge to force medication. I guess the Psychology Department had the judge on speed dial.

Another time a call for assistance came for the recreation yard. My friend and I were the first to reach the yard. She nor I weigh very much, small in size. As we reached the recreation yard, we observed two tall and very large muscular inmates fighting. We looked at each other, both saying damn in our minds. They must have thought the same thing because they stopped fighting and put their hands behind their backs. I had one inmate handcuffed when I realized the other officer didn't have any handcuffs on her. My mind was going crazy at this. What if the unhandcuffed dude jumped the one who was cuffed? Praise God other staff members arrived with handcuffs. She said that I had a look on my face that said everything, so from that day forward she always made sure she carried a pair of handcuffs. It's one of her favorite stories.

During the 4:00 count, one Lieutenant was in control taking the count. The other Lieutenant had a female inmate in the office, which meant she was counted in the office and not her housing unit. I mentioned earlier that when a telephone is off the hook for a certain (seconds) amount of time it sends out a call for assistance. When the phone in the office sent out a call for assistance, the Lieutenant taking count cancelled the call. A few minutes later he left the Control Center to check on the other Lieutenant. When he entered the office, the other Lieutenant was attempting to restrain the inmate who was giving him all she had. Once they were able to take control of her and placed her in handcuffs, she was escorted to SHU. He said that he didn't want to announce the call for assistance because he didn't embrace the other Lieutenant if it was a mistake. He said that now he felt bad because when he walked in the office and he was getting his ass whipped by a "girl." That had been an on running joke for years and still is.

It did happen again with the same Lieutenants but this time he said over the radio, "this is real, this is real." We were able to announce the call for assistance so he didn't get whipped by a "girl." That's why I loved the evening watch.

Chapter 2

*"Trust in the Lord with all your heart;
lean not unto thine own understanding. In all thy ways acknowledge him, and He will direct thy paths."*
Proverbs 3:5-6

Changes were coming: Word was out that a new Warden was coming and it was a female. Well now what will that bring? I wondered. There were changes and one of the biggest changes would be me.

I was in the Warden's office three or four times a month. Write-ups more than once. I was old school, doing it my way and the way I was trained, but now we were to be gentler and kinder Bureau. Old school teaching were out and kinder and gentler was in. Adjustments were hard but fair, but I remained true to myself. Inmates weren't changing so neither was I. I had a reputation of being firm but fair, which was not going to change. I remained that way throughout my entire career. Trust me, it paid off in the end. Inmates appreciated the fairness across the board. My attitude followed me my entire career. I was still fighting inmate crimes, breaking up fights, searching inmates and their property. Hell, I was even a member of the Institution Disturbance Control Team, no kinder or gentler here.

That year we needed to decorate the front lobby and visiting room for Christmas with Christmas trees, lights, and ornaments. There was even a theme: Disney wonderland. UGH!

Yes, I was responsible for that. Being me, I escorted a female paint crew to the front lobby to paint a Disney wonderland on the windows and handle the decorations. I must admit it turned out beautifully. I had a plane to catch early Monday morning for new Lieutenant training. Not having a chance to talk to the Warden about my decorating ideas before I left, I only hoped it met her standards.

On Tuesday morning, I received a call from the Warden while I was in new Lieutenant training in Denver, Colorado. I walked very slowly to answer that call, not knowing what was waiting; after all, she did call me in Denver. She was truly blown away with the outcome of the front entrance. The windows had been beautifully painted with the Disney wonderland. The overall decorations were over and above what she expected. So now I could go back to my training happy and get ready for what was coming next. On top of my regular duties, I was charged with planning and executing retirement party, birthday parties, staff appreciation events. You get the idea...

Why? Why? Why? Damn! Damn! Damn!! Now, I was the Social Director for Correctional Services (a self made title). One day after one of our big events, she introduced me as the person who planned the event and stated that I was a "people person." I turned around to see who was standing behind me. Was she talking about me? Me a people person? In all my life that was the first time I would be described that way. Remember, I was the black girl with a bad attitude and now I was a people person. What a long road I travel!

I learned that not all deals were made in the boardroom. I started attending institutional functions, family picnics, and Christmas parties. I even played softball on the institution's staff softball team. I was so busy I forgot that time had passed for my GS-11 Lieutenant

Chapter 2

position. Now I was receiving calls from other Wardens asking me to come and work at their institutions as a GS-11 Lieutenant. Where had the time gone? This time I would be leaving Lexington. It was time; I had accomplished all that I had hoped to do here at Lexington.

FMC, Lexington had a unit so far removed from the other housing units that today it is a female inmate camp. When I worked there, it was a part of the general population housing unit. Whenever there was a call for assistance, the entire group of officers first responded, including me, by looking at each other like we were on our to death row. Running to that unit was like running the New York Marathon. By the time we reached the unit, we couldn't breathe, let alone break up a fight. With all the huffing and puffing trying to catch our breath and the strength just to make it to the unit, some of them didn't make it. In most cases the inmates had broken up the disagreement. They were just as tired as we were. Unless they were trained for three minute boxing matches, they were tired too.

In this case, the officer had one inmate cuffed, but the other one got away. Listen to your gut. I spied an inmate mixed in with the other inmates looking on. He stood out no matter how hard he tried not to. I walked over to him and told him to turn around so he could be cuffed. He didn't say a word, just hung his head. I told the Operations Lieutenant, "That's him." As the officers were walking out with both inmates, we heard several onlookers say, "She got his ass. She ain't no joke." It just confirmed my gut feeling. Did I tell you that we had that same response almost every time we had to run to that unit?

Imagine running all the way out there and it would be a false alarm. That was the only time we found the energy to fuss and cuss while we were huffing and puffing. Funny, huh?

Once things had calmed down, one of the officers asked me how I knew it was him. My response was that it was a gut feeling, but he also had a wild look on his face. His eyes were bigger, he was still sweating, and his body would not him keep still (his adrenaline was still pumping). The inmates confirmed it as we were leaving the unit.

There was a lot to do when we locked inmates up in SHU, especially after a fight. Every responder had to write a memorandum on what you did or witnessed, and no two memorandum could be the same (court purposes). The property of both inmates had to be inventoried, packed, and transferred to SHU, along with the inmates. Yep, somebody had to go all the way back there, pick up their property, and take it to SHU, and it was not going to be me. The officer who pulled the alarm had to write a disciplinary report (detailing exactly what the inmates did), not just why they were fighting, but giving details like he/she hit her/him with a right hand to the face. Often times with more than one inmate involved, I would try to send an additional officer to help out because, with the exception of SHU, it was one officer per unit.

A serious note: Every staff member, whether you were in corrections or not, was equipped with some type of alarm for safety. Once that alarm went off, the Control Center was equipped with the right location of where the alarm had gone off. After receiving an all call over the radio transmitter, it was every staff member's responsibility

Chapter 2

to respond to that emergency: Trust me, when, not if, it's your time, you are going to want everybody there.

For example: If we had a fight in the gym. We have a in the gym.

There should be complete radio silence with the exception of the Operations Lieutenant. He/she was the only one who could clear the alarm and give out instructions on what needed to be done. We could not have all Chiefs and no Indians. There was one voice throughout the entire emergency and it was that of the Operations Lieutenant only. (See why I wanted to be a White Shirt? We ran the entire thing.)

Not for the faint of heart but they try anyway.

While working the evening watch, we received a call for assistance in the Special Housing Unit. On evening watch there should not have been any inmates out at the time. When we arrived at the unit, the #1 Officer was in between the sallyport doors. The way the SHU doors worked was the Control Center electronically opened the outer door to allow staff to enter the sallyport. Once the outer door was closed, the Control Center notified the SHU Officer #1 that there was traffic in the sallyport. The #1 Officer would come down and manually open the door going to the unit. At this particular time, the #1 Officer had locked herself inside the sallyport with the inner door key. From inside the sallyport, we could see two inmates fighting on the range or aisle (for non prison people), really going at it. There should have been a #2 Officer, but we didn't see her from where we were. After standing in the sallyport for a few seconds, the Operations Lieutenant had to override policy in order for the Control Center to electronically open the inner door and let us into the unit. Once we were inside the unit, we were able to take control of the situation.

I hope you were able to keep up because I'm not done. The #2 Officer had locked herself inside the inmates' laundry room because the #1 Officer had ran off and left her by herself, while the inmates were fighting. The #1 Officer said she opened the inmate cell doors because she thought they were the unit orderlies. (Orderlies were inmates who volunteered to clean the unit only in SHU.) Once she let them out, the fight began. And the rest was history.

Almost done: I got off work and was trying to go home. After a very long shift, I welcomed a warm bed. As I reached the parking lot, the #2 Officer was sitting on her car, waiting for the #1 Officer to out. Of course, I stopped to see what was going on. She said, "I'm waiting on #1. The bitch ran off and left me with them damn inmates fighting. I'm going to beat her ass." I told her to go home. She stated, "No! I am going to beat her ass, Lt. Higgins" I gave her a Direct Order to go home! She did or at least left the parking lot. Second situation done. The next we day we removed the #1 from SHU and reassigned her to another post. We could not have the faint of heart working in the inmate disciplinary unit and putting staff and the institution in jeopardy.

For the most part FMC, Lexington was a close-knit group. We were not above helping each other out, keeping each other in check, or at least attempting to keep each other in check. If I was doing unit checks and the officer was busy packing property because the inmate was locked in SHU, I would stop and help pack property.

Chapter 2

Someone would do the same for me.

On the morning watch after the officers had a long night of making rounds, counting inmates (three counts on morning watch), and sealing inmate mail for pick-up to be delivered to the mailroom, we would hear keys in the unit door. There would be an officer with a food tray delivering hot food to us that the Operations Lieutenant had cooked for the entire shift. We never went home hungry. He would say, "I cooked for the entire shift so if anyone tells it, they will be telling on themselves." I guess no one told because we ate the whole quarter.

In April of 1992 I was promoted from GS-9 to GS-11 (my goal: White Shirt).

Chapter 3

Federal Detention Center (FDC) Oakdale, LA

Back then everybody needed a foreign country under their belt. Louisiana was mine.

God had truly answered my prayers. All my hard work had paid off. I knew that the road ahead was going to long and rough, but I was ready. Oakdale, Louisiana, here I come.

My promotion included a paid move. So American Van Lines showed up, boxed me up and loaded me up. There was no GPS back then. AAA sent a mapped-out route to me. If you had a home that you couldn't sell, there was a federal program to purchase your house at fair market value. So my daughter and I were out. O! I forgot to tell you the best thing was temporary housing at any hotel for 45 days. Life was great!

Wait on it! Wait on It! I didn't know anything about Louisiana. It was a rude awakening for me and my daughter. When I moved, the Bureau hired a real estate service to help me with housing rental or purchase. The problem for us was we were black, so she would take

Chapter 3

us places that were not suitable for us. Every place we were shown was in the hood and across the railroad tracks. The houses were shanty shacks, run down, windows cracked, no grass in the yard. I expressed my desire and what I wanted and expected her to meet them, but it never got any better. After about a week, I called Central Office and explained my situation. As quickly as that afternoon they had a new realtor ready to go. Due to the time that was wasted on the first realtor, we had to extend our hotel stay another week. AWWW!

We finally moved into a beautiful home in a great neighborhood, where the person we rented the house from only cared about the color of money. His words, not mine. One interesting thing about the house was that while sitting in the study, I could watch the cotton grow, Yes, my neighbor had a cotton field in his backyard. Being in our new home, it was time to go to work.

Due to certain areas and not knowing the people, I chose to drive an hour to work everyday, even though I got stopped by the highway patrolman three to four times a month because of the car I drove. I was quite familiar with the phrase "Driving while black. I lived it. " To my surprise a lot of African American staff members drove an hour to work, so I wasn't alone. The institution was huge and divided into pods, open dorms with all nationalities and all security level inmates. My trials and struggles were about to get real.

My daughter was working at Sonic when she and the manager got into it. He told her not to look at him when he talked to her. My child lost her whole mind and part of mine. I was on my way to where she was, but she said she had it. BOOM went my mind. We were not from Louisiana and their ways were not our ways. That was all I needed to say.

I was shopping at Kmart. While checking out I was writing a check when the cashier asked me, "Honey to you have a job?" I wanted to say, "Yaw Bitch just hold the check until the first of the month." I just let it go unanswered.

In another incident I had a travelers check, and the person had to call a manager because they didn't know if I could use it or not. At least the manager apologized for the person's ignorance. My daughter left shortly after that. I was left all alone in this foreign country.

Cajun people are a very unique group who I fell in love with on sight. They are family orientated, hard working, mean what they say, and had my back from day one. Learning my way around the institution was not as easy thing to do. Inmate population, staff, how the institution was run were all different. I had my work cut out for me, but I was up to the challenge.

I do think Louisiana was one of the best institutions I've ever worked. I just loved Cajun culture and its people. A kind of people who went home after a long day of work and cooked dinner, then brought you some because you've never had it before. They loved their families and made me feel a part of that. Zydeco music and all the foods. I'm glad that was first move.

I spent one week on days for training and orientation and then it was time to go to work on my own. There was no other Lieutenant to watch over me to tell me what to do or how to do it. It was totally on

Chapter 3

me. I was the Senior Lieutenant. But I was ready. Of course I went to the evening shift, feeling a little nervous about being on my own for the first time. Inmate activity was routine, or so I thought. I still had a GS-9 Lieutenant working with me and loads of great staff who knew the institution and inmates very well.

The other Lieutenant and I had just finished rounds and had just entered the Lieutenant Offices when we looked out of the window onto the compound and saw fire coming out of one of the housing pods. It was in the Immigration and Custom Enforcement (ICE) pod. There was a full evacuation of all inmates, extra outside perimeter staff to keep the fence secure, and Administrators called in (Captain, Warden, Assistant Warden or AW) along with a recall of staff. Head count of every inmate and staff was taken. We had totally accountability. The Warden said, " Welcome to FDC Oakdale!"

WOW, my first week as a GS-11 Lieutenant was exciting. I found out the reason was Immigration and Customs Enforcement (ICE) was taking too long deporting some of the inmates back to their country. If this was the first week, I couldn't wait for the rest of my time.

Well before the next incident happened, I was able to get to know the staff and inmate population and get around the institution better. I was making rounds in one of the pods (inmate housing area) when an inmate fight/assault broke out. A call for an assistant went call over the radio from the unit I was already in. As I was stepping into the inmate common area to assess what was happening, an inmate ran toward me; someone yelled "That's him." I immediately stepped

Into the Shadow

in front of the inmate taking him down to the floor, just trying to hold him until additional officers arrived, which was in seconds. As the officers entered the unit, they spotted me on the floor wrestling with the inmate, they immediately came to my assistance. Once we had the inmate up and cuffed behind his back, a quick pat search was performed. He indeed still had the knife on him.

I will pass out later, I thought. We still had work to do. We still had to get this melee under control and get this unit locked down. We could not move the injured inmate until the unit was lockdown, for his protection. I had secured him in the Officer Office with medical staff.watching him. We had several inmates' involved and not enough staff. Finally after several minutes, which seemed like hours, we had all the inmates openly involved handcuffed and ready to be escorted to Special Housing. We didn't have the unit locked down because we only had a handful of officers left. The other officers were escorting the involved inmates to the SHU.

I was approached by a Jamaican inmate who asked me if the guys fighting had interfered with their recreational time. I told him if I could get the unit locked down, I would see what I could do in the morning. This guy then walked over to a group of Jamaican inmates, said something to them, came back to me, and said "Let's do it." I told every officer in the unit that had a cell door key to follow the Jamaican inmates and lock the door cell door behind each inmate as they went in. We were able to lock all the inmates down except one tough guy who refused to go in. I called my crew out and said "Let's go. Leave him."

Chapter 3

We were in the process of locking up the last of the Jamaican inmates who had helped us when Mr. Tough Guy turned around and saw the Jamaican guy coming toward him. He begged us to take him. So we met his request, cuffed him, and escorted him to the Special Housing Unit with the rest of his crew. The inmate did not sustain any serious injury, but it could have been if my staff had not responded promptly and correctly.

I knew I was in good when the Warden supported my decision and went against the Captain to give the inmates back their recreation time. Hell, my thought was I might need them again. The Warden said I had given them my word. It was fair; they helped us out and needed to be rewarded for it. Had it not been for the members of the Jamaican Posse, it would have gone horribly wrong for us because of the limited amount of staff on the evening shift. There was no way we could have gotten that unit locked down without the inmates. This was a unit where inmates were locked in all day until they were transition into the institution. It wasn't long after that that a Jamaican dudes made it to the yard full time. It didn't take long for me to gain the respect of staff and inmates.

Hurricane Andrew, August, 1992

I interacted with inmates all day every day, but nothing was scarier than preparing for Hurricane Andrew. We knew it was going to impact Louisiana, even if we didn't know where, we knew we had to be ready as best we could. Torrential rain and wind were so strong I thought we were going to blow away. It was awful. This was before Hurricane Andrew ever arrived. We placed the institution on 24 hour lockdown as we began to board up windows, move items off the yard, and tie down what we could. We were constantly making rounds, making sure the inmates had three box meals a day, some days even helping to make those box meals. All we could do now was hunker down and wait out the hurricane. We finally got the word that Andrew was downgraded to a tropical storm, but don't get it twisted. Winds could still be high as 75 m.p.h with torrential rains. It was better than a hurricane, and I was never so glad when this thing passed. I had not been home in 48 hours and didn't even know what my own home looked like. The institution only had minor damages and no injuries. We had an inmate evacuation plan in place, but we didn't have to use it. My daughter had moved back to Kentucky because she didn't like Louisiana. Thank God we made it and all was ok.

The Bureau of Prisons was very high on celebrating Correctional Worker's Week., and FDC, Oakdale was the best. Every year the FCI (which was next door) and the FDC (where I worked) would have an annual friendly softball game between staff, and every year the FCL would win. One of the rules was to have at least one female on the field as all times, so of course they had me play. I told them that I wanted to coach, not play. Not wanting to hurt my feelings, they all agreed. Yes, I was the coach, me! I could see why they lost. Can you say testosterone? The first batter for the FCI hit the ball so hard, 30 years later and I'm still looking for it. Have no fear we were only one point behind. The next time he came up to bat I called a

Chapter 3

timeout, had my catcher, pitcher and first baseman in and told them to walk him (testosterone remember). They didn't want to, but I was the coach, so they did it. It took them (FCI) out of their game since he was the only homerun hitter. I had a man on first base. I took him off and put a female runner in. Now it was time for my designated hitter. That was game. For the first ever the FDC won. Yea, I was picked up by the entire team and held up in the air. I took that one off my bucket list. I don't know if they won again because I transferred out before the next correctional week.

Strap in and hold on. I've got this.

Well here we go again. First, there were no females being promoted because it was an all male promotion board. Remember this was a male-dominated field and we were in Louisiana. Second, the Administration Lieutenant (who is responsible for the quarterly roster of correctional staff) did not schedule the females in those key positions because in his small little mind this wouldn't qualify them for promotions.

There was no policy that stated you had to work a certain post in order to be promoted. It just said you must be capable of working every post in the institution. For example: The Control Center was a critical post. Everyone should be able to work the Control Center. If the Administration Lieutenant did not assign female officers to the Control Center, you can't deny them a promotion. Each and every female was capable of working these posts; each and every female who applied for this promotion was well deserving. They had great work habits. They come to work every day and performed their duties to the best of their abilities without problems. At the end of this promotion board all three females were promoted to GS-8 Senior Officers. The last I heard, two of the females became GS-9 Counselors and the other one was a GS-Lieutenant.

There was a GS-8 African American male Officer working Control Center who wanted to be a Lieutenant, but was not being trained. I had his roster adjusted to my shift so I could give him proper training, the training that someone had given me. With help, he went on to become a GS-13 Captain and is now retired. We are still friends to this day.

Thank you God for the knowledge and courage to bless someone else.

> "Be strong and courageous. Do not be afraid or terrified because of them, because the Lord your God goes with you; he will never leave you nor forsake you."
> **Deuteronomy 31:6**

I became Special Housing Unit Lieutenant in the disciplinary unit. Inmates were locked down 24 hours a day, 7 days a week, with the exception of 1 hour of recreation time each day and three showers a week if they were good. Show your ass and we're taking that. Depending on your disciplinary status, you may receive visitation. When I was SHU Lieutenant, I treated the cell like it was home. If an inmate flooded his cell, spread shit on the walls, I did not move them out. WHY? So they can mess up another cell? No! If they messed it up, they stayed there.

One particular evening several inmates decided to pull a coup.

Chapter 3

They decided to break the sprinkler head inside their cells. When I went to the unit, water was all over the range and still running. The officers had already turned the sprinklers off, but sprinkler heads continued to drain out even after they were turned off. The officers had prepared other cells to move them into because that was normal for them, at least until I came. Walking through water as I entered the range, I advised each and every inmate that I was not moving them. They became very loud and further upset. "That cell is your home," I said. "If this is how you treat it, it's on you." There were water drains on the range just outside their cells, so there was no risk they would drown. Then they threatened to burn the unit. With all this water? Good luck!

As I was looking into the inmates' cells, it was funny watching these guys stand on whatever was in the cell to keep from getting their feet wet. Food trays, toilets, sinks, anything they could find, they used. I ordered the officers off the range to set up the video camera to record any further incidents. That's where I spent most of my night. After finding out that they were not being moved, however, the unit remained quiet.

The next day when I came to work the D/W Lieutenant was livid because I had refused to move the inmates out of their cells into dryer ones. He was waiting on me to do it because now the range was trashed. I was still not doing it. I guess the M/W Lieutenant may have finally felt the same way I did or he didn't have enough staff to move them, but either way they weren't moved. The range was not trashed when I left, but anyway an inmate could just be escorted down range and directed to clean it up. That is why we have inmate orderlies.

There was nothing in our policy that said inmates get another cell when they tear up the one they are in. As we were having a very heated conversation, the Warden and the Regional Director were making rounds, when the other Lieutenant began to complain to them about what the inmates had done and that I refused to move them. That Lieutenant was unaware that another inmate had informed the Warden and Director that, that particular group of inmates had planned and thought that because I was a female, I would move them. They were then going to refuse to go into another cell and take over the range. A coup.

Now the other Lieutenant was standing there looking stupid and getting ready to be schooled again. The Director told him the same thing that I had said: there was no policy that stated I needed to move them. There was also the fact that they had planned to take over the range had I moved them. Now the Captain was involved in the SHU meeting because he needed to be on the same page. What came directly from the Director's mouth was that no inmates should be moved unless the policy changed or during emergency situations only. Even if there was a fire, we had fire extinguishers and sprinklers on the range and in every cell to put it out.

At the time I think we had about 33 inmates in SHU. Eventually we were down to about three to five inmates. Disciplinary problems were improving on the yard. The word on the yard was when they went to SHU, they didn't come back out. The inmates couldn't figure out what was happening to the inmates when they went to SHU. Well, I will tell you my secret. They were being transferred to another facility or being deported. There was an escort tunnel from SHU to Receiving and Discharge (R&D). The other Lieutenants would take them back on the compound to escort them to R&D. I used the tunnel because it was easier and quicker, so the inmates on the compound couldn't see them leave. Therefore, they were confused as what we were doing with the inmates. Inmates were checking in but not checking out in their minds. Because of the disappearances, they stopped getting locked up. This shit was funny as hell.

The weather was more of a problem for me than the inmates. Louisiana had torrential rains all the time. One morning in particular I had gotten up for work only to find it had been raining all night. That wasn't unusual, but when I pulled my car out of the driveway, the front end was submerged under water. Panicking, I quickly pulled back in the driveway almost hitting the house. When I reentered the house, I notified work of the situation. They said, "Yes, we know. All of Alexandria is under water." No big deal. My house was built on a hill so we were safe including the car at this time. The street was completely flooded, and the water was halfway up the mailbox. My daughter was back by then, so I woke her up to help me watch the rain. While we were praying for the rain to stop; the locals were outside with their rowboats and water toys. OMG!

It was time to get the HELL out of Louisiana. Needless to say, it was time to upgrade my resume.

Watch God!

Into the Shadow

    I had put in for FCI, Memphis, to get closer to home. It had been a couple of months. The Warden from Louisiana had transferred to Memphis as Warden. There was a warden conference in Louisiana. He and the Regional Director took a tour of the FDC. While he was there, he had a conversation with me about Memphis. He had just demoted a GS-9 Lieutenant, he asked if I would like to follow him to Memphis. I stated that Memphis was one of my choices. He said that he had upgraded the GS- 9 position to a GS-11 and it was sitting on the Regional Director desk. The Director looked at me and said, "It's yours, if you want it."

    Goodbye, Louisiana! Hallelujah!

Chapter 4

FCI
Memphis, TN

In April 1994, I transferred to FCI Memphis, which turned out to be the biggest challenge of my career because of the type of inmates I had to deal with and the administration. My transfer had been pre-selected by the Warden and Regional Director. Normally anyone throughout the Bureau could apply for this position. There would be a promotion board which included the Captain, Associate Warden, Warden and a few others or a representative. They would review all applicants and discuss who was best suited for Memphis. Normally the Captain would have the deciding word. But in this case the position was upgraded from a GS-9 Lieuantent to a GS-11 Lieutenant. If the Captain knew about the upgraded position that meant he had his own pick. I was pre-selected without the knowledge of the Captain. So I came in on the wrong foot. When the Captain found out it was a done deal, especially when he had made a statement that no female would ever run his compound as long as he was Captain, he was totally surprised!

Into the Shadow

"For if God is for us, who can be against us."
Romans 8:31

Memphis was medium high security level institution back then. Gang population and gang activity was high. We had them all: Black Gangster Disciples, Latin Kings, Texas Syndicate, Mexikanemi, Black Guerrilla Family, Bloods, and Crips just to name a few. The gang members ran everything. it was all about control. However, there was a certain amount of respect they showed each other.

I was assigned to the evening shift. It was always my favorite shift. There was always a lot of action. Not if, but when it happened, it would be on the evening shift. Inmates were out of school, out of work, and just hanging out.

It was a usual quiet Sunday. The date was September 25, 1994, a date I will never ever forget. The Control Center made a call for assistance to one of the housing units. Upon stepping out unto the yard, I observed a group of officers and other staff members running behind an inmate. They looked like a bunch of Keystone Cops because whichever way the inmate ran that's the way they ran , it was a sight to see. Rather than joining in with the Keystone Cop route, I ran in a different direction in an attempt to cut the inmae off. I was then told that the inmate had a weapon in his hand. At this point I observed him throwing something on the roof of the chapel.

As I cut him off, I noticed several other inmates were now getting involved. The inmates had us surrounded as they began to assault staff, trying to keep us from cuffing up the inmate. I called the

Chapter 4

Control Center via radio to order a lockdown, all inmates report back to their housing unit and all Housing Unit Officers to stand outside their housing unit to observe any inmate activity or any other acts of violence. I also needed the Control Center to send additional restraints and videos cameras to me on the yard. I began to pull inmates off of staff, but it seemed the more inmates pulled off of staff, the more came to join in. At least that was true until the video cameras started running. After several minutes we had the institution completely secured and all inmates were off the yard with the exception of the one we were chasing.

It was show time! I looked at him and said, "All your buddies are locked down in their units. Now it's my way or your way, you choose, but either way you're going to SHU." He took two steps and put his hands behind his back. He was escorted to SHU without further incident.

He was a "Blood" gang member. The other inmates that joined in were also members of the Blood gang. The inmate who was assaulted was a Memphis-based inmate. The Bloods were trying to take over the Turf. Yes a Turf War over the institution, territory that already belonged to the Federal Government. Memphis-based inmates believed it was a matter of respect. To allow this group of young kids to come to their homes and take over was totally disrespectful and they weren't having it. So, yes, I had a total recall of staff. And, yes, on a Sunday you have to come to work because of this disturbance.

For the first time since working in the Bureau, I was shaken to see staff members being kicked and punched. Some staff members were on their hands and knees trying to get up as I was pulling inmates off of them. At one point as an inmate was charging at a staff member, I literally grabbed the staff member by his jacket and pulled him out of harm's way. This event got the best of me, but I still needed to put on a strong face for my staff. My nerves were completely shot. If I stood with my legs together, you would have heard my knees knocking. I needed a minute to get myself together. When the Warden came to the Lieutenant's office, I told him I had to leave. I needed to go home and get myself together before coming back.

I picked my grandson up from the babysitter and just held him until my daughter came home. By the time she got home, I was as straight as I was going to get at this point. Back to the institution I went. After all, we had a weapon on the roof of the chapel we needed to get off, which turned out to be a homemade knife, reports to give and write, paperwork, paperwork and more paperwork. We also had to identify all inmates involved. Several inmates were identified and transferred to other institutions.

With the exception of me, every staff member in the circle was hit or assaulted by inmates. Thank God there were only minor injuries to all staff members. The inmate who was assaulted in the unit was escorted and transferred to a local hospital. The Captain was shocked the I handled the incident as well as I did, and a few Lieutenants said that they were surprised. As long as I don't shock or surprise myself, I'm good.

Chapter 4

This incident went on intermittently for three days. Inmates were escorted to transportation buses because we had ran out of bed in SHU, as we waited on other institutions to arrive with additional buses. The inmates remained in complete restraints (legirons, belly chains, handcuffs and blackbox) on the buses until we were able to transport them to another facility.

When there was a disturbance in the institution, we had an independent After Action Review Team come in and conduct an investigation of the incident. Staff members from Central Office or other institutions came in and conducted interviews of all staff involved and any witnesses whether it's staff and inmates. If the investigation went bad, myself along with the administrative staff would be sent to another institution. We wouldn't even have time to pack our bags. They would just mail them to us.

Once the investigation was over, I was invited by the Warden to attend the After Action Review Team conclusions. These meetings include After Action Review Team members, the Wardens, both Assistant Wardens, Captain, but not me. Oh Lord, I wondered, where would they be sending me? I had just left Louisiana. Would I be going back? What the Hell!

When it was my turn, I walked in and was told to have a seat. This would be the time for a commercial break. As the Warden began to speak, my stomach turned and did flip flops. He introduced me as Lt. Higgins, the Operations Lieutenant who was working the day of the first disturbance in which several staff members were assaulted by inmates. Damn! Damn! Damn! Now they for sure knew who I was. I was as stiff as a board, too scared to move. Even if I had wanted to move, there was no way out. OMG!

The Warden continued to address me and the team members stating the obvious. Usually behind these types of incidents we all would be shipped to another institution and our furniture would follow us later, but after several days of interviewing staff and inmates she saved us all from moving to an unknown place. He further stated that he invited me to attend the meeting. After interviewing both staff and inmates, it was concluded that had it not been for me, we would have lost the entire institution. It was because of my calm demeanor and quick thinking that saved the institution. It was at this meeting that I found out the severity of the attacks on both inmates and staff, that all inmates had us surrounded with weapons. WHAT? Did I hear him right? Thank You Jesus! I didn't have to move to an unknown area in the Bureau. When he finished, I thanked them all for their findings. It was hard to believe that I saved the institution, but if that was the review board's findings and what the staff believed, then I was well with it. I wanted to skip out of there, but instead left praising God. All this was over some territory that already belong to the Federal Government, a prison, and on a Sunday.

> "No weapon formed against me shall prosper, and every tongue which rises against you in judgement you shall condemn. This is the heritage of the servants of the Lord, and their righteousness is from me, says the Lord."
> **Isaiah 54:17**

FCI in Memphis was fast paced with one incident after the next.

Chapter 4

While sitting in the Lieutenant's Office getting ready for mainline, when an inmate entered demanding to see the Captain, who was also getting ready for mainline. After several minutes of ranting and raging why the inmate needed to see him, the Captain stepped out of his office and told him to come in. When the inmate began screaming and threatening the Captain, the GS-9 Lieutenant stepped into the Captain's office to help subdue the inmate. All I could hear was bang, boom and other loud noises. The Captain's secretary looked at me and said, "I believe they are fighting in there." As I went to assess the situation, I observed three grown men and a lot of testosterone in the room. I leaned against the door of the Captain's office, trying to decide if I wanted to jump in to help or not. This is the man who refused to put female Lieutenants on the yard, and the other Lieutenant ran his mouth about being surprised at how well I handled the last incident.

Oh well, what the hell! I pulled up my pants to feel my imaginary balls and went in. As I reached for the inmate's arms to place them behind his back, he threw me on the sofa in the Captain's office. After a few minutes of this and knowing that mainline was getting ready to start, I couldn't open up food service or start feeding the inmates until this guy was in SHU. So being the only one in the room who didn't have testosterone, I grabbed the inmate's goody bag and told him to put his hands behind his back through his loud screaming and hollering. As the other Lieutenant escorted him to SHU, the Captain and I headed to food service. All the Captain bragged about was how awesome his Lieutenants were and how well everything went in his office. Inmates don't come in his office being disrespectful; we got something for them. BAH! BAH! BAH!. He talked like a proud dad for the remainder of food service. I was not impressed; however, I sure noted that he was a changed man after this incident.

> "The Lord said, I will make your enemies a footstool for your feet."
> **Luke 20:43**

I began to have more Acting Captain duties, learning more of the administrative side. Don't get it twisted. That didn't change the flow of the institution. I was making the rounds in SHU, addressing inmate issues when the call for assistance came out in SHU as a medical emergency. An inmate was laying on the floor in his cell unresponsive. Once we cuffed up his cellmate and moved him, we were able to go and administer assistance to the inmate. Keep in mind that I was Acting Captain and dressed in a business suit. I checked his pulse and realised that he was not breathing. It was time to kick off the red pumps and get busy. I began chest compressions. As the medical staff entered the cell, they started giving first aid, pushing air in his lungs with a handheld breathing apparatus. As additional staff entered the cell, one of my officers took over the chest pumps. I had never been so happy. Finally the outside paramedics were escorted to the unit. We continued our care for the inmate until the paramedics were set-up and ready to go. We knew that as they put him on the stretcher and took him out of the institution that he didn't make it. The inmate died, but I can say we honestly tried and did our best to save his life. I was teased for months by inmates and

Chapter 4

staff about me kicking off those red pumps.

Another officer and I started and co-founded a chapter of the National Blacks in Criminal Justice (NABCJ), Memphis Chapter. The purpose and mission of NABCJ sought to focus attention on relevant legislation, law enforcement, prosecution, and defense-related needs and practice-related needs, with emphasis on law enforcement, courts, corrections and the prevention of crime. It was also established to act upon the needs, concerns, and contributions of African-Americans and people of color as they related to the administration of equal justice.

We were able to bring together outside law enforcement agencies which included police and sheriff departments. State agencies included the state or highway patrol and other federal agencies. Our local mission at this point was to meet and greet local agencies and address all needs from all the agencies involved and to help them understand the rights and responsibilities of the Federal Prison System as it applied to the state of Tennessee. I can say it was very successful on all parts.

As a National Chapter, we went into the community to give back and give back we did. We were contacted by a local church in which a single mother of eight had left an abusive husband at Christmas time. She was in need of Christmas toys for her kids and food. Not only did the Chapter rally around this woman and her kids, but the entire institution rallied around her. We bought and received so much more than toys and food. We also took in clothes, coats and gloves. We needed two trucks to make the delivery. Once we got there, she was as overwhelmed as the rest of us, and we all cried. I was so proud of everyone at that moment to do something so selfless and to put someone they didn't know ahead of themselves and their families, especially at this time of year.

Through this Chapter we were able to bring a group of boys into the visiting room. Each was given an orange jumpsuit and placed in handcuffs and legirons at the beginning. Inmates were allowed to come in and talk about their lives, crimes they committed, and prison life experiences. Each child could ask questions and have an open conversation with the inmate about his prison life or crimes. As the inmates begin to talk about missing their family and the harsh rules of the institution, the boys begin to pay attention. You could see the terror in their little faces. Not being able to call or see their moms was too much for them, but you know you always have a few badasses that need to be broken down. So, I let the inmates deal with them on another level. They told them that they would see them later. The officers couldn't watch them 24/7. Their mama couldn't help them and terrible things happened when the lights went out. They also mentioned they would be locked in with other inmates at night. By the time we took the cuffs, legirons, and jumpsuits back, the boys were ready to leave. We served them pizza for lunch; some of them couldn't even eat. Their nerves were too bad a shape to eat. I know we saved a few, so the mission was successful.

We also adopted an inter-city elementary school through our National Chapter. We met with the school administrator to sign a declaration of adoption as to our duties and responsibilities, not only

Chapter 4

to the school, but to the students. Before any event, we provided the school with a list of names of who would be working the event. All of these duties had to be done on our off days or before or after our shifts. We patrolled the halls, sat in safe, after-school activities and school activities. We would talk to the kids. I would love on them and do whatever we needed to do to make them feel safe and supported. It was our school. We had a great partnership with parents, teachers, and the kids.

Lieutenants conduct monthly meetings with all department heads to discuss the need of the institutions and any departmental changes. The latest changes were for correctional services. Inmate moves would be done every hour, with ten minutes for the inmate to get from point A to point B. After the move was completed, all unit doors were to be secured until the next move. Any inmate caught in the unit or on the yard after the move closed would be charged with out-of-bound. No exceptions. Minor disciplinary sanctions would be enacted.

Once the department head meeting was over, we had a closed meeting for the Lieutenants and Captain. In this particular closed meeting, the Warden stayed to discuss SHU cell rotation, or the lack thereof. Inmate cell rotation was to be done on a weekly basis in SHU, which were not being done. The discussion was for me to take over SHU Lieutenant, not something I wanted to do. These inmates went hard, and starting cell rotation was not going to be easy since it would be the first time it was being done. In my mind I needed their support. I wanted to pick my own crew and use (OC) pepper spray, when needed. I knew the first two would be a possibility, but the pepper spray would probably be a big fat No. But I had to ask. My negotiations started. I made my stand and remained firm. The Captain opposed the (OC) pepper spray because he wanted to control when it was used, but the Warden gave me his blessing and support. So decision made, I had control of the unit to include gassing inmates who refused to rotate cells.

They wanted the cell rotation to be done on Saturday; however, any inmate that refused to move on Saturday would be moved first thing Monday morning. During the first cell rotation I came in to work, no one wanted to move. Hell, the whole damn cell house refused to move! I was mad as hell, due to the limited staff on the weekend I would have to wait until Monday to start the cell rotations.

Bright and early Monday morning we officially begin SHU cell rotation. First I had to set up my cell extraction team. A cell extraction team (CET) was made up of five or six officers, with one team leader and the others assigned to an entry position. The team leader in this case would me because I was the SHU Lieutenant. Any other time it would be the Captain.

Extraction Team responsibilities:

1. Team Leader (me) is the only person who may give the verbal command to both inmate and team members and disperse OS (mace) spray.

2. First person is the shield man and the first one in.

3. Second person person in will immobilize the right arm.

4. Third person in will immobilize the left arm.

5. Fourth person in will immobilized the right leg.

6. Fifth person in will immobilize the left leg.

7. Sixth person will operate the video camera.

8. Medical staff should stand by to check medical condition of the inmate being moved.

9. The Captain is there to observe.

As team leader, I introduced myself on video camera, giving the inmate's name and number and a quick explanation why and what we are doing. Each team member was introduced on camera before the helmet went on for full face frontal. He/she stated their name and stated whether they had any injuries or medical conditions that would prevent them from participating on the CET. They each stated what their responsibility or position was, which included the medical staff as well. Once introductions were completed by all members of the CET, the team went to complete silence, NO TALKING, all radios off. The only voice that should be heard was mine only for commands and instructions. No matter what was coming out of the inmate's mouth, the team should not respond because of legal issues.

Each team member was given a helmet with a face shield, jumpsuit and tactical gloves. Once I gave the command to cuff up the inmate so he could be moved to another cell, he could cuffed up or refused. If he cuffed up, there was no problem, he was moved without incident, but there's always that one. You know, the "Fuck You" guy.

I eat that shit (OC) for breakfast. Let's see if you do. Everything in SHU was done through the food slot. The cell door was not opened unless the inmate was restrained, even then it took two officers.

When I opened the food slot and dispersed the OS (mace) canister, within seconds he was coughing and down. I opened the cell door for the CET to go in and extract the inmate. At this point, the inmate was pretty passive. So restraining and removing him was easier than we imagined. Once he was removed, the inmate was placed in four-point restraint and the medical staff washed his eyes and checked the vitals. All of this was done on video tape for legal reasons. I would not remove a disruptive inmate without video camera. Once the move was completed, the CET once again went back on camera stating whether they received any injuries or not. Once that was done, the cell extraction was completed. The camera person was also introduced as the camera operator. Camera off.

For a four-point restraint, the right arm was restrained to the right side of the bed, the right leg was restrained to the right side of the bed, and the left arm and leg were restrained to the left side of the bed. The Officers needed to check on the inmate every 15 minutes until he was released from the restraints. Once the inmates had calmed down, he was placed in his cell until the next rotation. Having being tested more than once that day, all cell rotations were completed by the end of shift. They wore us out, but with no staff injuries, it was a great day.

After several more cell extractions, the Special Housing Unit began to get into a routine, not only on cell rotation but on the ev-

Chapter 4

eryday running of the unit. I should note that the National Training Academy was using my cell extraction videos as instructional videos on how to do a proper cell extraction. They might have gotten tired of showing my what-not-to-do videos. YAY me!

I can feel the winds of change and I'm going to need a coat!

The Puppet and the Puppet Master

> "Finally, be strong in the Lord and in his mighty power. Put on the full armor of God, so that you can take your stand against the devil's schemes."
> **Ephesians 6:10-11**

It was time for the Warden and the Captain to be moving on. Both replacements were straight out of hell. Satan spawn. We mixed like oil and water. As hard as they made it, I was still going to do my job and being the best I could be. Working with the Captain was like working with a puppet, and the Warden was his puppet master. What was that song?

"I'm your puppet. I'll do anything you asked me to. I'm your puppet." That's want they reminded me of. Whoever the Warden (Puppet Master) didn't like. the Captain (Puppet) didn't like either. The Puppet did his dirty work and I was part of it. All of sudden I was receiving write ups for whatever. My work ethic never changed, but I was getting written up two to three times a week.

On October 20, 1995, the Bureau of Prisons had major disturbances nationwide. Due the extreme damages of the prisons nationwide,the recovery period, lasted through December 1995.

News article from a Memphis newspaper:

The FCI Memphis revolt began at noon the same day. Approximately one hundred fifty to two hundred prisoners gathered on the yard, the only reason given in the report being to protest the congressional vote against rationalizing the crack laws. Another 200 in Unicor (Federal Prison Industries) refused to work, broke windows and equipment, and eventually joined the others on the yard. At about 1:00 P.M. demands were made, and rejected, for a senator, congressperson, and media to come to the prison. By 2:45 PM, fires in at least two units were burning out of control, Unicor had been trashed, and a BOP camera crew had been dissuaded from videotaping prisoners' actions. The command center ordered all staff members to evacuate the prison.

I was still SHU Lieutenant then. The unit was so full that there were inmates on the floor, with about four to six inmates in a cell. I went to the Captain and told him that I needed my regular crew back in there because the officers working there now did not know SHU policy or how the unit was ran. During the disturbance, staff were just assigned anywhere; it didn't matter what their regular assignment was, they just went where they were needed at the time. SHU was a very hostile and volatile situation. I could smell the danger in the air because of it being so over crowded. I made rounds three and four times a day and maybe more than that just to keep the unit calm. I went to the Assistant Warden over corrections to get the regular crew back in SHU to no avail. Finally the shit hit the fan. The officers were exchanging bed linens, and instead of the officer using the food slot, he opened the cell door. In an emergency situation like we were in, there should not have been a linen exchange anyway. That's why I needed the regularly assigned staff in there. Everything in SHU is done through the food slot: cuffing up inmates, feeding inmates, laundry/bed linen exchange, everything.

I was sitting in my office when a call for assistance came over the radio for Special Housing Unit. When the officer opened the door, an inmate came out of his cell attempting to assault the officer with a (homemade) knife. As I reached the range door, there were two Special Operations Response Team (S.O.R.T.) members standing at the range door. I had the officer open the range door. The two officers and I went down range. I told them to use their batons to get the inmate under control. By the time additional staff arrived in the unit, we had the inmate cuffed and back in his cell. An additional pat search was performed on the inmate in which we took another(homemade) knife off of him.

The Puppet and the Puppet Master pulled me out of SHU and reassigned me. I was told that it was my fault that the officer opened the cell door and did not use the food slot. Before I went home, I made a little phone call because I knew I was totally right in all I had done. I had taken the right swift corrective action to get control of the situation. That made no sense to me then and makes no sense to me now. When I made my call, I was asked what I did. I repeated back to him what I did. I was then told that I indeed took the right corrective action and for me to go to personnel (human resources) and have them send everything the Puppet Master had given them for the disciplinary actions he and puppet had just taken against me. Of course, I did what I was instructed to do.

Guess what? Personnel had no clue as to what had happened in SHU. She had me wait while she made the call to the same person I had just talked to. He told her she had 24 hours to have the disciplinary report on me on his desk. Did you hear me 24 hours! My SHU crew knew that for days I had been trying to get them back in the unit. I had written reports, dates, times and who I had spoken to about trying to get the SHU crew back in the unit. After the incident in SHU, all I heard from either one of them was crickets. No response just silence from everybody except the haters.

Now who was going in SHU because I was not going back? I expressed my feelings when I made my initial phone call and part of my conversation was that someone else needed to be assigned to SHU. I was not going back. I had done nothing and I felt I should remain on day shift with weekends off and he totally agreed. That had been my shift before the Puppet and Puppet Master pulled me out of SHU.

A week later I was called to the Puppet Master's Office He told me that he didn't have enough evidence to conduct an investigation so there was no need to take disciplinary action against me and that another Lieutenant would be reassigned to the Special Housing Unit. We already knew he was told to pull the investigation. There should not have been an investigation anyway. Remember he al-

Chapter 4

ready had taken disciplinary actions against me by pulling me out of SHU without proper cause. All of this was going on during a major inmate disturbance. Funny how my crew ended up back in SHU and didn't want to be there without me. Sorry guys, not coming back.

There was still plenty for me to do since the institution was on complete lockdown. We were into the recovery period after all we had two units to burn completely down, the units and unicor (inmate work area) trashed. There was an inmate property to be packed and inventoried, rounds to be made. I was good. I got what I wanted so back to work as usual. After long hours and hard work, we as a whole were able to restore the institution back to normal in a timely and efficient manner.

The Puppet was still coming for me, but when you are doing your job and the child of the Living God it's hard to, but it doesn't stop them from trying. The nonsense write ups continued to come. Now he and Puppet Master were really mad because they thought they had me. This time he went after my yearly evaluation in which I received an outstanding rating. He changed it to a fully successful rating with no rhyme or reason. Of course, I refused to sign it. I haven't had a fully successful evaluation since my probationary days. Human resources advised me to appeal it. I told them to leave it.

"Dearly beloved, avenge not yourselves, but rather give place unto wrath: for it is written, Vengeance is mine; I will repay, said the Lord."
Romans 12:19

Hard work defined who and what I was, not an evaluation. But I

Into the Shadow

do know that it was time to do something because the Puppet Master was trying to take my career. I needed to update my resume with a yearly fully successful evaluation. No institution was supposed to touch you with a fully successful evaluation. Hell, it's not even supposed to make it to the Regional Director's Office, but to add injury to insult, I had another GS-11 Lieutenant sign my resume. Usually the Captain would sign paperwork. He would then advise the Warden that I submitted my paperwork to leave or transfer out. Now neither one of them knew I had submitted my paperwork.

I made another little phone call to the Southeast Regional Director and told him a little of my story. To my surprise he already knew. I also informed him the Puppet Master was trying to take my career and about the yearly evaluation. I wanted out of the Mid-Atlantic region completely. He asked who the Puppet Master was. When I told him who, he said to give him thirty days and that he would personally inform personnel to fax my paperwork to him. Every time I made a professional call someone would run and tell the Puppet. I found out because the Puppet's secretary was my best friend. They didn't know the details of the phone calls, just the importance of it. I even had a hater Lieutenant tell me that I wouldn't leave because the Puppet Master and the Puppet would not voucher me out. I asked him why I would need them to voucher me when God has already done it.

It took about forty-five days from my initial phone call before it was announced: Lt. Higgins would be going to Tallahassee, Fl. What? Not some forgein country but prime real estate baby! The

Chapter 4

Puppet Master and his Puppet was so outdone that it was not officially announced. Several officers were so upset about how the announcement was handled until they finally made it official by announcing it on the front lobby marque. I wasn't bothered. I was out.

Now I was back on the evening shift. I'm good because it's my favorite shift. There was a Mexikanemi hit on Texas Syndicate. The Compound Officer called for assistance on the recreation yard. When I stepped out of the Lieutenant's office onto the yard, there were several small groups of inmate fights or assaults. One inmate was shouting out orders in Spanish. I knew I had to get him off the yard quickly because every time he said something another assault or fight would take place. At some point we had several inmates cuffed and placed in different areas of the yard until we could escort them to SHU. But I had to get the leader moved first.

As I approached him, I knew we were in for a fight. And fight he did. We were able to put him on the ground and put the cuffs on him from behind his back. I then had two male officers escort him to SHU. As I was walking away, I noticed some movement from behind me. When I turned around, he had broken loose or was trying to break loose from the escorting officers. Enough is Enough. I ran toward the officers and inmate full force, knocking everyone to the ground, including me. I hit him so hard that even he was shocked. Since the male officers couldn't handle escorting him to SHU, I had two female officers escort him and told him," If you even look like you are going to try something, I will embarrass you so bad I'll be the new leader. JUST TRY ME!"

He was escorted to SHU with no further incidents. Now it was time to get the yard under control. First thing was to lock it down, so we could get the Texas Syndicate gang members involved to medical safely without further inmate assaults toward them, since we didn't know who their enemies were. Once I had the institution lockdown, we were able to move them to medical safely. The Mexikanemi gang members were already escorted to the Special Housing Unit. They would be medically examined in the special housing, with no noted injuries. That day I placed seven Mexikanemi gang members (including the leader) in SHU. Normally the leader would not get caught; it would be his foot soldier, but not today. He picked the wrong shift and Lieutenant. I guess he thought the female Lieutenant was the weak link. He found out that I wasn't. Three Texas Syndicate gang members had minor injuries and were placed on protected custody and separate status from all other Mexikanemi gang members. The next day the word on the yard was that I looked like was on the WWE with that takedown. WOW! The WWE!

That was one week before my transfer to FCI, Tallahassee. The Puppet told me I needed to go to staff recall so I could officially get a "dat a girl." Any other time I would be very happy and glad to go. These guys had given so much grief, I didn't want anything from them, so I didn't go. I surely didn't want a picture with one of them shaking my hand. I was completely over Memphis, with one more act of kindness before I leave. I was approached by several staff members as they were leaving the staff recall that I didn't attend. They told me how much they admired me for standing my ground on all I had done and not attending recall. They knew that I had done an outstanding job handling the situation and the Puppet Master had to finally admit it.

There was an officer from SHU who was desperately needing to get to FCI, Ft. Worth.

I made a little phone call and asked the Warden at Ft. Worth to take him. He did so on my word. That was my last act of kindness in Memphis. Time to shut Memphis down.

With a week left, the AW of Corrections finally grew a pair. He approached me in food service on his late night and asked me if I needed anything. I told him peace and to be left alone. He had me put back on days for the remaining week.

When a person leaves any institution, the institution gives them a going away party to include a gift from the institution like a plague with the institution on it, mug, ink pen, etc. Once again I didn't go. My gifts were mailed to FCI, Tallahassee. So exactly one year from the inmates' disturbance in October 1996, I was transferred to FCI, Tallahassee.

Out of the Shadows!

To this day, long after retirement, I still will not recommend FCI, Memphis. If anyone asked me about Memphis, I would tell them to move on. Memphis is not it. Memphis saw me, you saw me, not a shadow of me, but me. You saw the promise, the potential, God's work in me and you were threatened by it and wanted my career. I had a praying mamma who would not let me fail. I knew my job and in spite of it all, I did it well. I guess I was supposed to blow cigar smoke up your ass and ask you how your day went, but I was not that type of gal. Never come at me half-ass. You half stepped when you came at me and that was your mistake because I got your ass in the end. To your shock and surprise, I knew the same people you did. So goodbye, Memphis. I wish you far better than you did for me.

"If God is for me, who can be against me."
Romans 8:31

Chapter 5

FCI
Tallahassee, FL

Tallahassee was an administrative security level facility, all female. Administrative institutions have all security level inmates from community to maximum custody. This is a very hard chapter for me to write because of some of the content, but if I'm going to tell my story I need to tell it. Keep in mind when females and male-dominants meet, it doesn't always end well.

Being at Tallahassee was like being a celebrity. Most of the inmates remembered me from Lexington. So, of course, they would drop by to say hi or to see if was true. Yes, Lt. Higgins was here in living color.

Things were moving at a slower pace, and coming from Memphis I learned to appreciate the pace. Female inmates were a different breed. Being a female, I could relate more with them emotionally. It was hard to see them as inmates because unlike male inmates, they don't have the roughness, the tough exterior. When I look at them I see our daughters, sisters, mothers, aunties and grandmothers. To see mother, daughter and grandmother locked up together is no surprise. The drug game ain't no joke. You have to keep it professional all the time, and that's why I made it this far, but I was human so I showed emotions. I gave out several hugs, hell, I even cried with them depending on the situation. I just thank God I had some empathy left after coming from Oakdale and Memphis.

I learned to perfect my golf game while escorting an outside construction crew around the institution. Monday through Friday, weekends off. When they worked, I worked. If they didn't work I didn't, so I played golf. All because an Officer said I called him a motherfucker. The Captain took his side. A few months later he was escorted out of the institution for the introduction of contraband. I got a helluva short game out of it. All good things must come to an end. The Warden said that he didn't bring me to Tallahassee to be an escort.

While standing mainline during the noon meal, I received a call from the Control Center that I was needed in SHU ASAP. As I entered the unit, the Officer informed me that an inmate had a noose around her neck and was standing on top of her toilet contemplating suicide. I informed him to notify the Psychology Department. Time was of the essence, she was screaming and hollering at me not to come in and was threatening to jump if I did. She had a roommate that I had to remove from the cell, so I used that as excuse to get the door open. At some point I had to close the range down and have outside staff removed because of their talking. With no Psychologist yet on the unit, I began to talk to her. During our conversation I

Chapter 5

learned that her son had just committed suicide, she lost her mother to suicide, but she still had her younger son and that was my in. She was feeling bad because she was not there for her son; she felt responsible for his suicide. My focus was that her baby boy visiting her in prison was far better than visiting her at the grave. He did not deserve what she was attempting to do. I stood on the toilet with her, not sure how I got there, but I did. By the time the Psychologist got there, I had cut her down. We both were crying and hugging each other. I gave her a piece of my heart that day.

Tallahassee had open dorms, so there was no way to lock down any of the units. This particular morning as I was reporting to work, two females were facing the wall in front of the Lieutenant's office. Neither one was fighting, but they were screaming or hollering at each other. There was no restraint and staff member near them. Obviously something was going on. I separated them and the first two staff that came by, I put them with the inmates to keep an eye on them. I then called control and told them to send me several pairs of handcuffs with the next staff member passing by. I still had my lunch in my hand. What the hell? Where's the morning watch Lieutenant? Simultaneously the M/W Lieutenant showed up and there was a call for me to come to a certain unit. I left as the Captain was dealing with the inmates on the wall who weren't cuffed. As I was leaving with several handcuffs stuffed in my waistband, I heard the Captain say, "Somebody go with her." When I reached the unit, the inmates were raising hell about one thing or another. Once I entered the dorm, the officer who the Captain sent after me started putting cuffs on whoever, per my orders, they began to calm their asses down. So, my first question was "why are you still on the unit and not working?" Crickets!

Now I had to figure out how to get their attention. I couldn't lock them down per say because SHU was not big enough to hold them. So, like the great mama I was, I ordered every inmate to their bunk, to be quiet. I didn't want to hear a beep. As I took the handcuffs off of the ones we restrained, the Captain walked in and asked about my plan. I told him this was it. Every inmate would be restricted to their bunks until further notice. I would assign an extra officer to help with bathroom breaks because all inmates would need an escort. If the unit team needed an inmate, they would need to come and get her, no exception. Anyone causing any further problems would be escorted to SHU, without question.

This was at 8:00 am. When I thought about them again, it was mainline time and they were next to be called on the rotation. I looked at the Captain and remembered I forgot about them being on bunk restriction. He said they would be alright and they could go to work now.

I know this shit sounds crazy, but you can't make this up. Looking back this shit was funny as hell! Hey it worked, 75-100 inmates in time out for half a day and not causing any additional problems, I'd take it.

It all started with a wedding y'all. One warm Saturday evening the inmates decided to have a wedding. Full dress, minister, wedding party to include a maid of honor, bridesmaids, groomsmen,

Chapter 5

the whole shabang. I don't know how they pulled it off without staff being aware or maybe staff was aware and didn't care. Not on my watch, but Monday evening, I was hit with it first thing. This is when the inmates started calling me soft walker because they couldn't hear me coming. I learned as a rookie to always protect my keys. I would always tuck them in my pocket, a habit I never changed. I was so afraid of losing my keys and that is a whole other book.

It took me five days to walk down all the players including the bride and bride. Any type of intimate relationship or sexual encounter was an automatic transfer. Everyone directly involved was escorted to SHU to wait for transfer to another institution. I received a call from SHU that one of the brides needed to talk to me. She began to tell how the wedding took place without being interrupted. An officer had allowed it because the officer was in her pocket. She went on to tell me that she had proof. There was another female on the yard holding all the evidence for her. I told her if she indeed had proof to have her friend drop it at the gate of SHU because I was not going to look for it or hunt it down. She asked me to come back to SHU in an hour. Not believing her story, but giving her the benefit of the doubt, I played along. After informing the Officer in charge of SHU of what was going on, I left. After completing my rounds I went back to the SHU gate and DAMN there it was, approximately $1000 worth of contraband, makeup, perfume, hair product, just to name a few. So with a name and the product, I immediately informed the SIS Lieutenant (Special Investigator Supervisor).

I completed a Change of Evidence form, completed my shift

and went home. The next day before shift, I received a call from the SIS Lieutenant. I was told to pull the inmate out of her cell, give her a phone call and provide her with a pager number. She was to call the officer and give him the pager number to call her alleged cousin (who was a federal agent) coming through town, so the alleged cousin could pay the remaining balance of $1,000. The officer would then bring the remaining merchandise inside the institution to give the inmate. Everything was done as instructed and guess what? His dumb ass got busted on the way to work the same day. Stupid! Stupid!

I know you think this is the end, but it's not. A couple of hours later I received a call from the Control Center that I was needed in the front lobby. Two females were there to see the warden. As I was coming through the gates, she was inviting them to her office, which was a no, no. I could smell trouble all over them. This was not a peaceful visit. We all went to the Warden's office. I knew this was not going to end well. It was the wife of the officer who had gotten busted earlier with a friend, wanting answers that she was not going to get. After being told several times that there was no available information at this time, she was told to wait for her husband to get her answer. Tension raising, I decided to end the meeting. They looked at me like they weren't going to leave. I was now on my feet (I felt like I was back in Memphis). You in my house and you're thinking you're not leaving. It's a question of how because leaving was not an option. And that's what just came out of my mouth. I just pulled up my pants to feel my imaginary balls. Realizing that they didn't

Chapter 5

have an option, they chose wisely and decided to leave. Still feeling uneasy about the entire situation, I escorted them out and returned to the Warden's office to have a conversation, but as I entered her office she apologized to me because she realized the danger that she had put us both in.

Standing inside food service on the evening watch, I noticed that a certain Case Manager was not present. He was one of those people who always stood mainline on evening watch, so you would notice if he wasn't there. No problem for me, so I continued mainline. Once it closed, I completed my rounds in all the housing units, went to the Lieutenant's office, and worked on paperwork. Sitting in the office the Case Manager who was missing in food service was on his way out. He would normally stick his head in, but not this time. I knew something was not right. I just thought he had something going on at home. About 15 minutes after he had departed the institution, an inmate entered my office who appeared to be very upset, crying hysterically, stating to me that she had just been raped. The inmate medical center was right across from the Lieutenant's office. I escorted her over there and placed her in the examining room with the nurse watching her so I could isolate her from the rest of the inmates. When I interviewed her, she stated that the missing Case Manager was the one who raped her. I called my other Lieutenant to inform him of the situation. It was confirmed through the Control Center that the Case Manager had indeed departed the institution and I instructed them to pull his office key and not to hand it out without permission from me. Then I called the SIS Lieutenant and the Captain to inform them

Into the Shadow

of the situation. ALL HELL JUST BROKE LOOSE!

The inmate did not back down from her story and agreed to be escorted to an outside hospital to complete a rape kit, but I had to go. She didn't trust anyone else. However, once the outside Federal Agency showed up to interview her, I asked to be dismissed. This guy was a friend of mind. I am an emotional wreck. Then it was my time to be interviewed because she said it happened during mainline. So I had to confirm that he was not in mainline and the only time I saw him was when he was leaving. Did I have a conversation with him at all? NO. With keys to his office released, they took over his office, cut the chair cushion right out of the chair, and DNA testing from the rape kit confirmed that sperm was there, his or mot don't know. I don't know who I felt worst for him or her, or maybe both. It was a very hard time for me and my other Lieutenant because we couldn't talk about an ongoing investigation. I didn't know if he was guilty or not. I just knew he didn't return to the facility for the rest of my time there. The inmate was eventually transferred to another facility.

Still on the evening watch, the Special Housing Unit officers accidentally opened the cell door of a maximum custody inmate. Max custody inmates have to have two officers and a Lieutenant and full restraints (handcuffs, black box, belly chain, padlock and legirons). Here I was looking down the range and the inmate was in the middle of the range bobbing and weaving like Muhammad Ali. It was a great thing that I knew the inmate otherwise we would have had a bigger problem. As I entered the range, I asked how she was

Chapter 5

doing, how long she had been in Tallahessee, and why was she out here looking like Muhammad Ali. We laughed about the Muhammad Ali joke as she entered her cell without incident and stated that she didn't know why her cell door opened, but she had to be ready in case someone tried to do something to her. Not on my watch. She knew that and like most females there she trusted me.

From that day on, she showed her butt on every shift that I was not on: flooding her cell, screaming and hollering all shift, giving the officers a hard time. They were already afraid of her because of her custody level. Well, here is the kicker. She wanted me in SHU, so she told the Warden if he put me in SHU she would stop. Guess what? I was SHU Lieutenant for two years until she was transferred to another facility. I didn't mind it. It was just that SHU was always a mess when I took over. I was a policy person, that's how I survived in the trenches.

First I started with her cell. She was a max custody inmate with soda cans, cases of water, hair products, body lotions, vaseline, and other regular commissary items. So, we compromised to get all the stuff out of her cell. Her commissary would be kept in my office, soda would go in a cup, and water would be a trade out (Example: if she had five bottles water in she cell, she would need to give me five empties for five full ones). The other stuff was placed in a shower caddy and only used when she was in the shower and then placed back in my office. All things had to be done on day watch with me. I had recreation put a stationary bike in the SHU legal library so she could get some recreation or just to get her out of her cell for at least an hour.

Things were going well. I had several female inmates in SHU because of staff/inmate investigations. This one inmate told me while I was making daily rounds that she was under investigation for staff allegations. She said that a male staff member told her that she could never get away from him because she was an inmate and he was staff, accessible to all areas of the institution. She further stated that he would bring in a work crew and that was his excuse for getting in the unit. Even with that, officers should not have let him in SHU. He would stand at the front of her range and whistle a tune to let her know that he was in the unit. She stated that she was beginning to fear that he would eventually come down the range and try to do something to her. When I spoke to the officers they knew he wasn't supposed to be in SHU, but he told them if he left they would have to supervise his inmates work detail because there was no one else to do it. The SHU officers were too busy to watch the outside work detail. Thinking they had it all under control, they allowed him in but his slick ass wasn't on the range, he was harassing her from the range door, which I found out later was locked, which meant that was as far as he could get. My crew was always on point. The Captain, AW, Warden, SIS Lt., his department head (his boss) and I had a meeting and the Captain and the SIS Lt. interviewed the inmate. She told them the same thing that she had told me. At this point, he was moved to the Camp were we housed male inmates with a written memorandum noted in the Control Center that this staff member was not allowed back in the institution. That took care

Chapter 5

of his nasty ass.

I spent days trying to think of incidents that did not include inmate/staff investigation. I'm sure there were many but the staff investigations outweighed everything else. I remember my GS-9 Lt. losing his hair because of stress. We couldn't talk about inmate/investigations because you put the investigation at risk. Inmates came to me because I protected their names. No one knew who gave me the information; they just wanted to live and do their time in peace. Even if I had to lock them up in SHU to protect them and the information, they were ok with it. I had three days to complete an investigation of any infractions, so that was the excuse I used with the Captain's knowledge. On the third day I would release them back to the compound.

Except, always an exception, the unit team was conducting unit moves. This inmate did not want to move in with her grandmother, so I moved her to another bunk. She didn't want to be in that one either. When she came to mainline she gave me her reason for not wanting to bunk with that inmate. That inmate had heroine in a teddy bear. She had been using all weekend. She was upset with me because she said I should have caught them, I should have noticed because they were high all weekend. How is she going to be mad at me, but she was. I told her after mainline to refuse to move to the unit officer. I would place her into SHU, for refusing programs (which was refusing to move) until Monday, at which time I would release her. I had an officer go the inmate's bunk who supposedly had the heroine and take all the teddy bears in her room, complete a confiscated property form, and make sure the inmate signed it. If she did have heroin inside the teddy bear, she just signed stating that it was hers.

Once I had locked up the informant, all hell broke loose. Her mother came into the office like a freight train. "Why is my daughter locked up? You better let her out cause I'm going to lock up this whole damn compound. Lt. Higgins, why did you lock up my child?" It took me a minute to calm her down. Man, I thought I was going to have to fight that big woman. Once I explained to her the situation about her daughter's room change and the alleged heroin inside of the teddy bear, I told her that I would release her daughter on Monday for refusing to move. As the mother was leaving my office, she said to me, "Your word?" I shook my head yes. Knowing my word was good, she left the office. So, I notified the SIS Lt. about the teddy bears and he asked me to cut them open. NOPE not doing it, too much paperwork if the drugs were in the teddy bears.

Sometime Monday before my shift, I received a phone call stating that one of the teddy bears indeed had heroine inside the stuffing of the bear. I needed to come in early and sign a Change of Evidence form. Four inmates were locked in SHU pending investigation of a narcotic. Each inmate had to drop urine for a drug test to see if they were using. I don't make this shit up. So, of course the word came to me that they had used someone else's urine. Proper procedure stated that inmates wash their hands, spread their legs, squad and cough, pee with the door open while the officer watched. Not fun for either the inmate or staff, but that was policy. I sent word to the

Chapter 5

SIS Lt, that his girl got beat, the inmates had used someone else's urine (UA). The UA were re-administered on my watch, myself and another female officer redid the inmate UAs, sorry you couldn't see their demeanor when I pulled them out of their cell to pee, again. Lt. Higgins we already dropped a UA, but whose did you use? Was my question, you know they came back dirty, I didn't even have to tell you that. Yes all four were charged and transferred to another facility.

I left a piece of me with the women in Tallahassee. I saw your fear, your pain and your guilt when you were out there slinging that dope for your dope-dealing man, hanging out with that gang banger, staying in that abusive relationship, mom and dad living that life, so you're living that live, that's all you knew. You're a single mom working all day and night just trying to make it and still there is too much month for the money. You're out on that street corner trying to make enough money to get that next hit of dope, wouldn't know your dad if he was standing next to you.

Federal Agent knocking on your door. You knew that was coming. The federal prison doors slams shut, reality check. Child Protective Services is taking your kid. Maybe they will go to your family or maybe not. Now they are in foster care, and you worry if you will ever see your kids again. Some of you won't see them until they are grown with children of their own. Some of your children are buried so deep in the system you can't find them and others were adopted out to other families, but then there are those who start living your life starting that cycle all over again. I saw your fear. I felt your pain

Into the Shadow

and tired to help with your guilt because at the end of the day you are still a mom. Now you begin to ask yourself the same question I asked you: What if?

Throughout the five years I was in Tallahassee, I was Acting Captain more times than I care to count. The move into reservation housing for quick availability to the institution (part of the first responder team). Spending four out of five days on the inmate transport bus transferring inmates to Miami FDC because of an inmate food or work strike. Going to Washington D.C on the inmate transport bus because Lorton Correctional Services was shutting down and inmates were being transferred to Tahallassee. Transporting an inmate to FCI, FT. Worth, Texas, in a Winnebago because her medical condition would not allow her to fly. I was on so many airplanes transporting inmates I could been an airline stewardess when I retired. Then there was helping to provide Christmas for more than 20 families every Christmas for the last two years.

> "So the last shall be first, and the first last: for many be called, but few chosen."
> **Matthew 20:16**

Once again I made a phone call to leave and this time I needed to be in North Carolina. My Captain in Tallahassee was being promoted to a GS-13 so he was leaving. He and I both agreed that I needed to leave also. I felt that I had accomplished my BOP goals and I decided to get married and retire Lt. Higgins. She was tired y'all. He lived in North Carolina. The Warden at FMC, Butner was

Chapter 5

the person who was very instrumental in hiring me into the Bureau. He followed my career from beginning to end. I started my career with him and now I would end it with him.

Chapter 6

Federal Correctional Complex Butner, NC

In October 2001, I transferred to Butner, North Carolina, a Federal Correctional Complex which consisted of four facilities in one area. There was the Federal Medical Center, Federal Correctional Institution (medium), Federal Prison Camp, and Federal Correctional Institution (low).

This would be the final chapter of my career. This was a necessary move but a very hard move for me. I am completely out of my element. Butner was a male inmate medical hospital of all security levels for inmates with special health needs. It had a full hospital facility specializing in oncology and behavioral science. Many medical and surgical specialties held clinics and performed procedures at the FMC. It had the only residential program devoted to the treatment of sexual offenders in the federal prison system. This was truly a hospital with all housing units on the inside. I was used to the wind and the sun on my face from being outside Now when I went to work, I didn't know what the weather was like until I left work.

Chapter 6

But that would be the least of my problems. Working with mental health inmates was going to be a super challenge for me. I was very nervous and stressed walking around in those corridors of the hospital because mental health was so unpredictable. One minute everything was fine and the next minute all hell had broken loose. The FMC was not any different. There was always threat of suicide, flooding the cells, staff assault attempts and self- mutilations. I learned that like everything else, communication was the key. Once I started making rounds and talking to them on a daily basis, my attitude began to change.

There was one inmate who always threatened suicide. He would put a noose around his neck and stand on a chair. After responding to several of his suicide attemtps, I started talking to him on a daily basis. He had made several attempts to ask for a Lieutenant or a supervisor, but no one ever showed up so he started putting the noose around his neck to get their attention. After this conversation with him, my outlook changed. No more nooses around your neck on my shift. I told him if he needed to talk to me to just tell the officers and they would notify me. The last time he did this on my shift, the officers notified me without an emergency being called. When I arrived on the unit he had taken the noose off and was sitting at his desk. He wanted me to know that he would be leaving soon. He had received his transfer notice and he had appreciated me talking to him. He was soon released from SHU to the general population.

One day while I was making rounds, he asked me what time I got off work. I told him the time I got off without questioning as to why he needed to know. The next day when I came in to work, one of the nurses told me that the same inmate had asked her about the time. After she told him the time she further stated to me that all hell broke loose. He had showed his natural born ass, but he wanted to make sure I was off duty. Yes, Lord, that's why I talk to inmates while making rounds. That was his last hoorah. He was transferred soon after that.

In the same unit there was an inmate who shit and smeared it all over his walls, pissed on the floor, flooded his cell, just acting all kinds of crazy. I didn't make inmate cell changes under these circumstances. If you wanted to live in shit and piss all over your cell, have at it. His water was cut off due to his flooding the cell. Supposedly when he used the bathroom, the water would be turned on so he could flush his commode. That didn't work because he used that opportunity to flood his cell and the range. I was not familiar with this inmate, so I didn't know his pattern.

When I received a phone call from the officers that we needed to do a cell change, my response was "I'll be there in a minute." Upon entering the unit, I was informed about what was going on and that this was what he did on a weekly basis. I then proceeded to the inmate's cell where I informed him that he would not be getting a cell change. If that was how he wanted to live, that was on him and not my officers. Needless to say, the Day Watch and the Captain were furious. So what? They would have to get over it, and they did. My response was to ask why I would move him into another cell just to mess it up. I wasn't doing it. They looked at me like, Damn, why

Chapter 6

didn't I think of that? But it was too late. The Day Watch Officers had already moved him. Oh well.

That night when I made rounds I purposely stopped by his cell. The inmate asked me to turn his water back on. My response was "Why? You don't drink water and you obviously don't bathe in it, so why would you need your water back on?" I further asked him why he was pissing and shitting on the floor of his cell and smearing it on the wall. "A dog has enough sense to shit outside his house," I told him. "A dog doesn't sleep where he shits." Since I had his complete attention at this time I pushed a little further. I told him that he had played crazy for so long that he was never going to find his way back to reality. If he continued to act crazy, that would be his reality.

After my two off days, an officer approached me and stated that I had done what the psychologists couldn't do. That I had cured him and he was in the general population. While I was standing mainline, he was waiting on me. He actually thanked me and said that he was trying to beat his charges or get a reduced sentence. He further stated that if anyone messed with me, they would have to answer to him. Well!

I was making rounds as usual, when an inmate stopped me to ask a question. The conversation was getting long. I had to get him out of my face without him knowing I was trying to get him out of my face. (Don't forget, I was dealing with special needs and mental health inmates.) I was standing by the unit elevator when the doors opened. After about the third time this happened, I jumped into the elevator telling the inmate as the doors closed that I had to go. When

I reached the main floor and the doors of the elevator doors opened there were two inmates standing there laughing their heads off. They said, "Lt. Higgins we were trying to help you. We kept sending you the elevator." Now I was laughing my head off because I didn't know what was going on with the elevator. I had finally taken it as a sign and jumped in. It should be noted that the two inmates at the elevator are the ones I just wrote about. Man, we came a long way.

While standing mainline, an inmate approached me and said God told him to tell me that He was going to make a change in my life. I thanked him and he moved on. I didn't question it. If God could make a donkey talk... (Numbers 22:28). A few days later he came back and said God told him to tell me that He is going to make a change in my life. Once again I thanked him and he moved on. I was on the morning watch when this all occurred. A couple of weeks later, I received a phone call from the Warden (It wasn't unusual for him to be in the institution since he worked all hours). He asked me to come to his office when the 12 o'clock count cleared. When I arrived, he explained to me what was going on and if I would mind switching institutions and going to the FCI. He had that Lexington connection so I didn't mind at all. That connection made us family. After all, God had told me that He was going to make a change in my life.

FCI Butner Medium

I was off to the FCI, which was where I was most comfortable. I was at home, and it was just next door or down the road.

Chapter 6

Butner was one of those institutions that was laid back and had more sophisticated inmates. Inmates were just doing their time without problem for the most part. They were mostly old school inmates just wanting to do their time and get out. Don't get it twisted. There were still fights, sexual assaults, but most of the time that was during the night time. When we turned the lights on, no one was snitching or telling. Everybody "fell in the showers." Butner was notorious for inmate sexual assaults, and no one would tell because of fear. I watched inmate behavior; I prided myself on that. I noticed how an inmate would enter the prison and then after several weeks his behavior changed. He didn't walk as tall or wasn't as loud. His behavior and personal hygiene would change. His hair would grow a little longer, pants a little tighter and his walk was a little bit softer. Some of them would go into protective custody but there were the ones who would remain on the yard and deal with it. It was a conversation between staff, but if the inmates wouldn't snitch or tell, that's all it was, talk. It was a place where the inmates called me crazy but the officers called me Queen and the Executive Staff called me Captain.

I received a call that an inmate was standing on a chair with a noose around his neck and the psychologist was attempting to talk him down. I had the officers go ahead and set up the video camera and that I was on my way. When I entered the range all I could hear was the psychologist screaming and hollaring that the inmate was going in four point restrainsts and that he would be placed on suicide watch. How in the hell was I going to get the noose off his neck? I had my officers escort the psychologist off the range and had a cell extraction team suited up in case I couldn't talk him down. I promise you all I said was "Get your ass down. Black people don't commit suicide." He got down and said, " Lt. you're right. I'm sorry." I can't make this shit up. Since I had the video camera running I didn't need to explain why I had the psychologist removed from the range. They could review the tape.

Butner was a place where the officers performed their jobs with little or no supervision. A place where they knew without a doubt that I had their backs and I knew that they had mine.

I needed to be at a mainline every day. I needed to be there to observe inmate movement and activity. The Compound Officer ran mainline. He called out all the work details and unit to eat. Yes, there was protocol. Every week we were provided with a different rotation list. If I ran late, the Captain would run her ass out there and start calling mainline instead of letting the Compound Officer do his job. Normally I had the officer to relieve her. On that particular day, I told him not to relieve her. I was sick of her jumping her ass out there every day like were not doing our jobs. She ended up running the entire mainline which could run anywhere from an hour and a half to two hours, depending on what was being served and if they had enough food. If that was the case, more food would need to be cooked and mainline ran longer. The Officer wanted to relieve her, but I dared him too. Lesson learned, she never did that again. We all knew our jobs and didn't need someone trying to demean what we do, not even the Captain.

Another time I was working the evening shift. I had come in

Chapter 6

early to work on paperwork because I was so far behind. Just before getting started on my paperwork, I heard this loud cursing coming from the compound. As I looked out of the office window, I saw an inmate in the Captain's face cursing her out. He was talking to her like some bitch on the street. I stood there for a few minutes to see if anyone was going to show up to assist her, even though there was a GS-11 Lieutenant standing there with her, no one reacted. God always puts you where you need to be. I needed to work on paperwork, but I went onto the compound to get this inmate out of the Captain's face. I stepped in front of him so he could focus on me and take the attention off her. When he found that he was getting locked up or going to special housing, he took off running into the Captain's complex. Yes, the same person he was cursing out he now wanted to protect him. Not today. I didn't give up my paperwork and come out here in this heat for his salvation. Today your ass is gone and is not coming back over here. As I was heading to the Captain's complex to get him, I was joined by the same Compound Officer and another female Lieutenant. In an attempt to reach him before me, the Officer pushed a mop bucket in front of me in order to slow me down. It worked because I had to side step so he was able to reach the inmate first. By then I was so zoned out they had to call me three times to bring me back. The Officer and I put handcuffs on him and escorted him to R&D (Receiving and Discharge) to be transferred to SHU. Once what happened hit the compound, all the inmates were saying "She told him that if she ever locked him up, she would come and get him herself." She kept her word.

Once he was transferred to SHU, I made several phone calls to ensure that he was not coming back over here. To my delight he had flooded cells and staff assaults or attempts on several occasions. Him coming back was over here was not an option as that point.

I received "Supervisor of the Quarter" for that quarter. I can't remember what all I did to get that honor, but I do know I was tired and worn out. "Supervisor of the Quarter" was on my bucket list, but somewhere I had lost the list.

The Unit Team, case manager, counselors, etc, would have unit potluck lunches or order lunch in and any left over they would try and drop off at the Lieutenant's office for the officers. During my shift I wouldn't allow them to do it . They would need to take it somewhere else. My thoughts were invite them to your unit for lunch and stop dropping the scraps off that you don't want. These officers are protecting you every day and this is how you repay them? Is this how you treat first responders? Dogs and slaves ate scraps. We know longer had to eat the massa scraps. I conveyed my feelings to the Officers and the next day bought lunch for the entire shift. The Officers working the units were relieved in order to get their free lunch. That was how it was supposed to be, not dropping off scraps from the master's table.

In July 2006, I retired from the Bureau. Butner was my very last stop. My mother was dying from complications of cancer and asked me to retire. All this happened because someone planted a seed 20 years ago. I thank every person who turned me toward the sun, those who watered me, those who feed me, and even those who threw the

Chapter 6

dirt because without dirt I would not have grown.

To apply for a government position, visit www.USA.gov.

Chapter 7

Inmate-Staff Manipulation

I would be remiss if I didn't touch on the subject of inmate manipulation toward staff. It always started out with something as simple as a five minute conversation. It didn't just start with them asking you to bring in contraband into the institution. First they needed to see if you were "weak enough." Inmate term, not mine. When I was asked, "What's your first name?" My response was always "Officer." "Why is it that you don't smile?" My response was "You go over there and ask that male officer the same question, then come back and ask me." I didn't pass any of my tests, the simple questions to see if I was grooming worthy. But, trust me they didn't stop with me.

They found someone else who they could groom and so it began. You have become too friendly and you don't even know it, but he/she does. You eat lunch every day at your desk and notice that someone has left you a soda, the next day soda and chips. You know who it is, but you choose to ignore it because now you are feeling special. During your conversation, he/she knows that you're single

Chapter 7

or your man/woman has mistreated you and how lonely you are. All that inmate sees is your vulnerability. Yes, you told them all he/she needs to know about your personal life. You don't see anything wrong with it; after all, he/she is locked up. All these inmates have is time, 24 hours, 7 days a week to convince you how sincere they are. He makes you feel like you are Halle Berry, and she makes you feel like you are Denzel Washinton because he/she already knows that you have no to low self-esteem. So, now your looks are changing. You are wearing make-up, your hairstyle is different, and you are walking just a little taller.

Then the inmate demands get bigger so you start bringing items into the institution. You are so caught up in the fantasy, that you put his/her life ahead of your own. Sorry, life as you know it is over. He or she promises that no one will ever find out. Today is the day when the institution decides to do staff searches. You knew when you stepped through the front door they were looking for you. There you are with a bag full of whatever contraband the inmate has asked you to bring in. You are now wondering how the institution found out. If only the two of you knew about it, and we know you didn't tell it, who did? You just got a reality check; the fantasy is over. THE INMATE ALWAYS TELLS.

Another Officer and I were counting a housing unit. Counts are always double counts in all areas of the institution. One person counts while the other person stands at the front of the range, looking down range and watching for inmate movement (there should not be any movement, talking, no sounds at all). Once I finished my one, we would switch places. I would stand and the other officer would count. This was not a stand up count, which means they could be in their rooms as long as you can see flesh and they were breathing you were good. Most inmates stood up so we could finish count and they could get back to what they were doing.

This particular inmate would lay in his bed every day during the count. When I approached his cell he would pretend to be asleep, but he would have a little bit of his penis sticking out from under the cover. I continued to allow him to do it until he had it all out. On this day, I let the other Officer count first. When we both had finished counting, I asked the other Officer if she noticed any inmate with his penis out. Her response was"No"! I told her to hold her position as I went back down range. I called that inmate out in a very loud voice, so the other inmates on the range could hear me. I talked about his little tired ass piece of meat and told him, "If I ever come down the range again and you have that little tiny piece of meat out, I will have your ass locked up for that thing being so small. My nine-month old nephew is bigger than that, and you are proud to show to show that?" I left the range laughing all the way to the Officer Station. The next day when I reported to the unit to count, he was not on the unit. The other inmates had teased him and talked about him so badly that he checked into protective custody. I didn't pass my test. Had I continued to allow him to show me his penis, he would have eventually approached me because he thought I was okay with it.

Another time, at the very beginning of my Bureau career, we were transitioning from inmate personal property to institutional

Chapter 7

uniforms. A female inmate entered the Lieutenant's office stating that her bag of jewelry was missing out of her locked locker. As I was walking to her unit to investigate, I noticed that indeed her locker had not been broken into but yet her jewelry was missing. Doing what I do, I applied the heat on the compound (where inmates hang out), in order to get her jewelry back. Inmates don't have inmate locker keys. You feel me. The next day the same inmate came back to the Lieutenant's office with her bag of jewelry and dumped it on my desk. She thanked me and said if it wasn't for me, she would not have gotten it back. She said to me, "We're cool. Lt. Higgins, just pick you out one. I'm not no stitch. Nobody will ever know. You know I'm not like that." I told her, "Thank you, but no thanks and you are welcome. What I am going to do is lock this stuff up in the confiscated locker and in the morning you are going to walk your happy behind back over here and we are going to the mailroom and mail it all out." Having said that, I gave her a receipt for her items.

Another female Officer and I worked the 6am shift. Upon arriving to work, we had to check into the Lieutenant's office to let them know we were reporting to work. Every day when we reached the Lieutenant's office there was a female inmate in the office, the same inmate every day. The other Officer and I tried to do the right thing and look out for him. We pulled him up on it. We tried to tell him to be careful of the inmate and how it looked with her in his office every morning, but he wasn't listening to any of it. After that, when we came to work, we had to report into the Control Center because he was not in the office. We had tried, so at some point we decided to leave it alone and just kept moving. It wasn't long after we tried to help him, that an official investigation took place and photos of him were found in the inmate's locker. The other officer and I were caught up in his mess. We were officially interviewed as to what we saw or witnessed, signed affidavits on what we said to him and anything else we may have known. Because he fought it, we had to go in front of a Federal Judge and testify under oath because of something that someone else had put us in the middle of. This is how strong of a hold a manipulate inmate has on you when you allowed them in.

How do you go home and tell your spouse that you lost your job because of an inmate relationship? Not only that, but that inmate is pregnant? He got caught because during the investigation a money order was traced back to him. He supposely sent the inmate's family a money order to pay for the abortion. True or not, he was fired. This was over 30 years ago, so tracing a money order wasn't so hard. How do you face your family?

Staff manipulation can sometimes be just as bad or worse than inmates. While working at Memphis, I received a package in the inmate mail room. The mailroom staff called to notify me about the package and told me that it was from a former inmate. They worked with inmate mail every day. I know they knew the policy; Special Investigation Services (SIS) should have been notified instead of me. So, I told them to send it to the SIS because I was not coming. These people called me for months but I never went to get the package. Why they didn't follow policy and notify the SIS or return the package, I don't know, but I never picked the package up. Total staff manipulation.

Manipulations are very easy to get into, but hard to get out of. When and if you do get out, the cost will be too high. It not only affects you, but your family as well and the people you work with. The best way to avoid inmate manipulations is leave all your personal stuff at home, be a professional at all times, and wear a look of confidence in all you do.

Chapter 8

Affirmative Action and Harassment in the Highest Form

When I mentioned Affirmative Action was alive and well, that is an understatement. As an African-American female working in an all-male-dominated field, I found it was not as easy task. At least Eddyville addressed it when they let me know early that Affirmative Action was the reason for me being hired, but it couldn't and wouldn't save my job. Affirmative Action numbers only show the hiring process and not the firing process.

So, when I went up for a promotion and a white girl was chosen over me with less experience or the blue-eyed blond was taken completely off the yard always from all inmate population because she was screwing one of the Captains, I couldn't get angry or upset because I had already been told that the only reason I was there was because of Affirmative Action .

There was a female officer who worked for the state who was sexually harassed by her supervisor. When she complained, nothing was done. She eventually sued them and won her case and they paid

Chapter 8

her a lot of money. Even after the lawsuit, he continued to be her Supervisor for at least another six months to a year, until the complaints started again. The dude is still there. They just moved him to another area away from her. They are both still working there. Total male dominance.

By the time I started working for the Feds I had found my voice, so I didn't get a lot of harassment, sexual or otherwise. I would stop mine at the first sign.

However, I am a witness to females suffering in silence. I won't name the institution because of the sensitive nature of the subject. I was at the end of my shift. It was one of the rare times I was on day shift. I was just getting ready to walk out when Control called and asked my 10-20 (location). I had an urgent phone call. As I began to talk to this person, I could tell by this person's voice that something was terribly wrong. Upon getting the Captain's attention, I told him that I needed someone from the Psychology Department.

This was a female officer who was thanking me for always being kind and supportive of her. Now I panicked just trying to keep her on the phone until the psychologist arrived in the office, which was within minutes. He had to write his response on a piece of paper so she couldn't hear his voice. I was repeating whatever the officer said out loud so he would know how to have me respond. She was contemplating suicide because she was being seriouly harassed by both male officer and male inmate. She had walked in on a bad situation between the staff and inmate and was afraid to tell because of the threats and harassment. She couldn't afford to give up this job and her former job didn't pay enough money. She felt that she was in between a rock and a hard place.

The Psychologist had me to talk her into the institution. I personally didn't think it was a great idea, but it was all we had and he was the professional. It was the longest wait of my life. The Captain and I both needed a Psychologist at this time. When she finally reached the institution, I was never so happy in my life to see a person. I met her on the steps of the institution with the Captain and the Psychologist. She turned on me and said that she had trusted me, and I had betrayed her. I was upset at first but then I was glad she had come; hopefully he could help her.

Just as I was heading out of the institution to leave for the second time, the Psychologist called me and the Captain into the conference room where they were. She wanted us to hear what was going on. That's when we learned the extent of her situation. She had actually told her mom to pick her son up from school and she had laid all of her important papers (insurance policies, etc.) out on the bed, She was done because she didn't know how to handle a situation that someone else had put her in. The Psychologist thanked me because of my quick action and response. I hugged her and we were both crying, Needless to say, her situation was handled the very next day. She continued to be under my watch for the remaining time I was there.

As I said in my Memphis chapter, I was terribly harassed by the Warden (the puppet master) and the Captain (puppet). I can't tell you how I did it because I don't know. I couldn't change the

Chapter 8

fact that I was born black or female. I just knew that I had to face that shit everyday. On evening shift, the puppet would wait; on the morning shift, he would come in early. I requested a meeting with the Mid-Atlantic Regional Director, it got somewhat better but now much. I don't know if it was because I was black or because I was a female. I sugar coated that shit when I talked about it earlier in the chapter, but that shit was alive and well. I felt like the puppet master had a black nanny as a child that looked like me and she whipped his ass on a daily basis. So he took it on me and anyone who looked like her. I remember when he had me under that fake ass investigation, I had a GS-11 Unit Manager as my representative to witness what was being said and make sure the meeting was fair and impartial. After that the puppet master treated him really horribly, took his unit away from him, and moved his wife to the camp. I tried to apologize to him for getting him in that mess, but he said I didn't owe him an apology. He told me the puppet master was trying to send out a message for anyone who was trying to help, meaning me.

This type of hatred is pure evil and this is who we had as representative for the Department of Justice, the watchdog for other agencies in the United States. I just realized the extent of his hated right now as I am writing about it. Evil, just pure evil, and I lived with it every day.

The puppet didn't have any balls or was afraid of losing his own career and did whatever the puppet master told him to do. None of that shit made any sense to me. It showed prejudice at the highest level. That's one reason I never wanted to be a Captain because you will never dictate to me how to treat a person. But me being me, was not an easy take down. Anybody else would have felt broken.

The secret to this was I had a praying mama. My parents had prepared me for this type of person my whole entire life. They raised me with a right and unbreakable spirit. Never let anyone see you sweat, if I needed to cry do it in private, but keep it moving. So, every day for over a year I came to work with a stronger face and made up mind that these two assholes would not break me and they didn't. They tried, believe me they tried. This was not like it was a secret society, the puppet master and I had a meeting with the Regional Director and they did some little investigation and interviewed staff. Of course when the investigation was over, there was no negative feedback. In the end it was just a few disgruntled staff, but the institution and the puppet master were good. The biggest problem for me was they were angry or upset because I wouldn't allow them to break me. Keep in mind I was the only female Lieutenant, period, so I was strictly on my own. I told you what he did to the Unit Manager who represented me just as a witness. They never hired another female Lieutenant the entire time I was there. Food for thought!

They tried it, though!

"I will praise thee, for I am fearfully and wonderfully made."
Psalms 139:14

Chapter 9

The Dangers for a Female Correctional Officer

Working in a prison setting is one of the most dangerous things I have ever done. I always had to watch my back and tried to have an exit plan. It was important to be aware of my surroundings. Stay where someone can see me, preferably the Control Center cameras. I never allowed an inmate to crowd my space.

While working at Eddyville, I would always leave SHU as the general population inmates were being released to the yard. I had to go through the general inmate housing unit to leave SHU. I always chose that time because the unit doors were open and I didn't have to wait for the officer to let me out, but the problem with that was the inmate cell doors were also opened at this time. One day while making my way out of SHU through the general population unit, an inmate was in his cell waiting on me and said, "You need to stop coming through here when the cell doors are open." Lesson learned. An inmate could have pulled me in his cell and no one would have known because of the lockdown system back then. The inmate cell doors were opened and closed simultaneously. The officer would announce by mouth the the cell doors were opening and a few minutes after the same announcement by mouth that cell doors were closing. He didn't even need to check on a door unless a red light came on in the Control Center. So, yes, I changed what I did and how I did it.

I developed a habit while working in SHU of holding onto the range door bars as I opened up an inmate cell. I did this to steady myself so I could see when the inmate door opened and closed. There was flexiglass attached to the bars for protection. One day as I was releasing the inmates out for rec., an inmate approached me and tapped on the flexiglass where my hand was holding onto the bar. He didn't say anything, he just walked away. Another lesson learned. It should be noted that both of these guys were from my hometown. At anytime an inmate could have smashed my hands in between the bars and flexiglass. Ouch! I told you that I was in over my head at Eddyville. My problem is not one officer ever said anything to me about the dangers I had put myself in. It took inmates from my hometown to school me.

Right after I found the escapee in the woods who was standing behind the tree looking like the Incredible Hunk, he stated to me that at some point I was close enough for him to grab, but he decided against it. I was by myself until I caught up with other officers. Male dominance was everywhere with no safety measures in place for females.

Before I was hired by the DOJ, I transferred to another Kentucky state facility. I usually don't talk about this facility because I only

Chapter 9

stayed a week. It was a minimal security level (camp) facility, but some of the inmates still has a lot of time left to do. I reported to the evening watch, and I was given a flashlight and radio. I was told the radio may or may not work; it didn't. I called Shift Command, (this is where the Supervisor's office is located) which might or might not answer the phone. So, here I was, in a dorm style inmate unit and no one had checked on me since I reported to work. What the hell? No one even made rounds in the unit.

Then you heard "lights out." This is why you needed a flashlight. The dorm would go completely black. Pitch black. Thank God it was count time because I knew that there was somebody there besides me. We counted with flashlights, although we were not allowed to turn the lights on for count. How important could that count be? It was their rules, not mine. I left after a week, not even a week (5 days). I didn't return after my off days. I had a bunch of sick leave so I went out on sick leave. I felt that this facility was a set-up for me and other female officers to fail because of the male dominance. They felt that because we were female and you should be able to handle what they were doing.

In fact that is true. We can and will do it when given a fair chance!

This facility had no level of security or safety checks. They left females in completely dark open dorm units with 40-50 inmates with no safety measures in place. Who puts a female in a dark ass anyplace with 40-50 males and expects her to be or feel safe with a flashlight? For my own safety, I resigned. I purposely didn't mention or say the name of this facility because my daughter went to work there not so long ago and not much had changed, she also resigned.

At the same facility when you pulled into work, you parked your car in front of the housing unit where you were assigned to work. Inmates walked up to you and asked if you wanted your car washed or if you were having car problems. If so, they would fix your car for you. No barriers or safety measures for anyone, especially females. Total set up for failure for female officers.

When working with federal inmates, I was locked in the unit with the inmates. At 10:00 p.m. after the count, the unit door keys were taking off the until. So, being a female or male you were locked in, but the difference between state and federal was with the Feds, I had a radio that worked. It had a body alarm on it, a telephone when left off of the hook would sound an alarm for assistance and even with the lights out, we had safety running lights on the floor. We could still see inside of the unit and I could always turn the lights on if I needed to. There was little to no danger.

Chapter 10

The Dangers of Inmate Escorted Trips

Escorting inmates was the absolute danger to everyone involved, male or female, and it was the worst thing that I ever did. Any time an inmate was removed from the institution, the dangerous intensified; all of your protective barriers were gone. You didn't know who the enemies were or where they were. On a normal day, we often took inmates out of the institution, in full restraints. Two officers with weapons rode in the vehicle with the inmate and another vehicle escort came behind the first vehicle with weapons. This was known as a chase car. I don't think that needs an explanation.

I had to assist on an inmate funeral trip out of the state, and of course we had to fly. We had the inmates in restraints (handcuffs and legirons), and we were issued weapons. This was my first out-of-state funeral trip. My nerves were on high alert. When we walked in the airport, you can imagine all the looks, stirs, and whispers. I probably have done the same thing in the past. Everyone thinking that she was a killer, however, we did get to board the plane first.

As we were boarding the plane, the pilot took our weapons and sat us all the way in the back away from the other passengers. Once we made it to the funeral, all the family and friends wanted to hug, kiss, and visit. They were upset when they found out that we had to sit away from all family and friends. They were really mad when they found out that after the funeral we had to return back to the airport with no funeral dinner. My nerves were so shot on this trip, I stood up during the entire service. Remember it was my first time, but I can honestly say my nerves never got any better on other inmate trips. I never sat down. I was always vigilant because the moment you become complacent, what you expect to happen usually does.

There was the last funeral trip that I went on and was not the Senior Officer. The Senior Trip Officer on this trip removed the inmate restraints at the airport. Once we reached our destination, she allowed the inmate's family to bring the inmate's personal clothing to the church so the inmate could change into street clothes. After the service we went back to the inmate's home and had dinner before going back to the airport. I never told, but like everything else, word got out and eventually she lost her job long after I was transferred. Never Ever Again will this happen to me. After this trip I was Senior Trip Officer or I didn't go, just that simple. I mentioned earlier that I was a policy person; that's how I survived all that was thrown at me.

After that trip, I made a statement that soon got out. If you don't want it told, don't do it in front of me. I don't care who or what it is. DON'T DO IT. I talked about inmate/staff manipulation and this is staff-on-staff manipulation in the highest degree.

Chapter 10

Funeral and bedside visit trips were the only inmate trips that inmates were supposed to be aware of because the family had to be contacted about the arrangements for the trips. An inmate bedside visit was when a member of an inmate's immediate family was critically ill and was not going to make it and chose to say their goodbyes rather than wait for the funeral. Inmates were allowed to do both. I had only escorted one bedside visit. The inmate was a community security inmate, which meant I was the only officer escorting, no weapon, just a set of handcuffs in my pocket.

She was allowed to wear her personal clothes. I wasn't bothered with any of it because I knew the inmate. Her mother was gravely ill and the inmate chose a bedside visit at an out-of-state hospital. Once we arrived at the hospital I didn't need to do anything. Her father had it all worked out. He had the room cleared out so the inmate could have a visit with just her and me in the room. He had food brought to the hospital waiting area while the other family members were visiting her mother. Once we finished, we exchanged places. At some point I told him to relax because it was all good. Before it was time for us to leave, they asked me to pray for her and her family. That was the best honor she could have given me. Her father gathered up all the family who were there. We all held hands with the father standing by the room door winking at me, letting me know that once again he had it. Once the prayer was done it was time to get back to the airport and back to Tahallassee, FL. My heart bled for her or anyone in that situation, but at least she got to see her mother before she closed her eyes for the final time. I appreciated her father because of the way he handled the family to ensure his daughter had a calm and peaceful final visit with her mother.

When medical trips were compromised, these trips were cancelled and rescheduled because of the outside dangers. There were no family visits or phone calls when an inmate was admitted to a local hospital unless there was prior approval by the institution, all for staff and public safety and security.

When I was preparing an inmate (female only) for a trip, I personally conducted the strip search to ensure my and my partner's safety. I needed to make sure that it was done properly and that there were not any unknown issues with the inmate trip. Inmates were not allowed to take anything out or bring anything in. When we took out a male inmate, he would need to be strip searched by my partner (who was a male) to ensure our safety. Even if someone else said that inmate was stripped, we did appreciate their help, but we did it again. That's just how I was. You can't be too safe or secure.

That actually happened a lot, where an office would tell you that they had already strip searched the inmate. That's what happened on this incident. I was taking a community custody inmate out for a doctor's appointment, which meant I was just dropping her off. She did not need me to stay with her. Once again, I was told that she was already strip searched. Remember my motto: I do my own strip searches. As I was stripping her out, I got to the squat, spread, and cough part. Well, when she coughed, money in a plastic bag fell to the floor, straight out of the pocket book or her purse. That's what I call a vagina because the female inmates can put so much in that

Chapter 10

thing. Where the hell did that come from? Inmates can't go to the ATM and I thought she had already been strip searched. That's why I do my own. The only trip she was taking was to SHU.

When Lorton Correctional Services closed down in Washington D.C, we needed to go to D.C and pick up the female inmates and bring them back to FCI, Tallahassee, Florida. When I did things out of the ordinary, I chose my crew: officers who knew how I did things and who I could trust to get it done right. Upon arrival to the facility, we were told that inmates were already strip searched and were ready to go. My crew and I started reaching for gloves and went to work, stripping the inmates out. I thanked the Lorton staff for all their help, but we needed to do it ourselves, for our own safety. It was a long ride back to Tallahassee. During this searching process, one of my officers called me because she needed help with a huge-busted inmate. The problem was the officer was allowing the inmate to hold her breasts up her with hands. She couldn't see because the inmate was using her hands as a shield to cover anything she was trying to hide.

Now, let's try it the Lt. Higgins way. I had the female spread her arms out like she was flying and bend over like she was trying to touch her feet or the floor. When she did that, her breasts were swinging like a swing on the playground. Child, when that wallet opened up, everything fell out. Money, lipstick, a marijauna cigarette, a few pills, you name it, but more important than that was the look on that female officer's face as she was looking at me and then at the inmate. She said she had never seen anyone do that in a strip search. I explained to her that the way she was doing it, by allowing the inmate to hold her breast (wallet) up with her hand, allowed her to hide the contraband under her hands.

Once again we found a little bit of everything, nail polish, lipstick, money, etc. because a female put anything in her vagina (her purse). Once again the inmate could not take anything out or bring anything in without prior approval. The very moment you become complacent is when it happens. Remember purse (vagina), breast (wallet). It was a long ride back to Tallahassee!

Chapter 11

The Oath

I, [name], do solemnly swear (or affirm) that I will support and defend the Constitution of the United States against all enemies, foreign and domestic; that I will bear true faith and allegiance to the same; that I take this obligation freely, without any mental reservation or purpose of evasion; and that I will well and faithfully discharge the duties of the office on which I am about to enter. So help me God.

This is the oath we take as Correctional Officers. Not all correctional staff are bringing contraband in the institutions, but that's all the news media report. We report to work when no one else does. You hear a lot about federal furloughs in the news. I've worked through two, one without pay. I have spent nights at the institution because the weather was so bad I couldn't get out and the officers/lieutenants relieving me couldn't get in. In the situations, it doesn't matter the rank because we cover whatever needs to be covered. As

Into the Shadow

correctional workers, we do it in order to get the job done.

The Bureau received intel that an officer stepped on a prayer rug, during Inmate Ramadan services (whether he did it on purpose or because he didn't know the customs) he lost his life. His family did not send that young man to work to lose his life. He did what he was told to do.

Another intel stated that while an AW was standing in mainline addressing an inmate problem, an inmate sliced his face. The only time an inmate could see executive staff was in food service while they were standing in mainline or making the rounds on the yard. I have never allowed the executive staff (Warden and AWs) to be a yard or food service without coverage. I always walk them or made sure someone did if I was tied-up I would walk in front of them or the walk back them, even the SHU I would have my #1 officer walk with them or at least stand on the range or aisle (for my non-prison people).until they left SHU. The warden made a joke out of this at my retirement party stating when Lt. Higgins ran her hand across her throat, it was time for them to get off the yard.

I had an Officer ask me why I did that and no other Lieutenant did. My response is that it was my responsibility to protect them and to make sure they were safe. I just felt so bad for that AW, that I made a private vow to myself that it would never happen on my watch.

So, I pulled inmates off of staff, left red pumps on the range, cut an inmate down during a suicide attempt, came to work when I was too tired to move and put up with all the crap for the oath.

Chapter 12

Summary

"Deliver me not over unto the will of mine enemies: for false witnesses are risen up against me, and such as breathe out cruelty. I had fainted, unless I had believed to see the goodness of the Lord in the land of the living. Wait on the Lord: be of good courage, and he shall strengthen thine heart: wait, I say, on the Lord."

Psalm 27:12-14

Looking back I never felt the dangers or the stress of being in Corrections because I lived it every day. I now know that Corrections is one of the most deadly and dangerous careers. I put my life on the line every single day, without hesitation or thought. I made a commitment to protect and serve, but it was more than that. I loved what I did and I did it well. I loved the challenge of the job with both inmates and staff. I learned that like life you pick and choose your battles. Don't sweat the small stuff.

The moment I put on my uniform, I was transformed. I became the uniform. I stood just a little bit taller, my back became a little bit straighter, my mind became just a little bit shaper. It was all about the respect of what I was and who I represented. My Officers started calling me Queen B, that's what I became when I put on my uniform. I left all personal business locked in the car. Always the professional, I never got caught up in gossip or drama. I stayed on my course. I loved Correctional Services and it loved me back. My favorite saying was "If you cut me, I will bleed Correctional Services."

I had been in the shadows for too long; it was time to come out. I'd been okay being in the background. Now it was time for me to lead, take charge, and make my voice heard. Once I put my mind and heart into it, I came out of the shadows. I knew I was coming out when all unnecessary drama started happening to me.

My parents had instilled in me strength, never to give up. It didn't matter what someone else said about you, it was what you say about yourself that mattered and to always be a leader. They were not raising followers. One of my mom's favorite sayings was "If everybody jumped off a bridge, would you?" When someone comes at you because you're black or female it's their problem, not mine. I experienced all of it including two furloughs, one without pay. I chose to not let any of it get in my way. I stayed focused and continued my journey.

Doing these trials, I made a little bit of history, I was the first female at that time to find an escaped convict while working at a maximum security institution and the first female Lieutenant to work at FDC, Oakdale. After that I lost count or stopped counting because I started counting heart prints because of the people that I touched or the ones who touched me. Everything that I experienced was a part of my purpose, and I wouldn't have changed it for the world. I would go back to the Bureau today if I could take my whole crew with me. I became a threat. Someone saw my purpose and knew I had a plan, didn't think I had what it took to complete my journey. The one person they didn't count on was God. He held me through it all. He knew I would stay on my course and finish this race. I had too much to lose. Now when I look across Central Park and see those white shirts standing on the steps, I see me!

The sacrifices I made were many; however, they weren't just mine, but my family's also. My career was so demanding that I often neglected my home and family life. Thank God my daughter was in high school and didn't need a babysitter. There were times I needed her to stay with my sister because my hours were so long. I remember my daughter coming home one night and the lights were out. She called me at work and told me that the lights were out. I had been working for so long that I forgot to pay the light bill. I wasn't concerned. I just told her, "Write the check and pay for it." From that moment on, she was responsible for paying the bills in the house.

She used to refer to our home as FCI, Higgins because of my strict rules. I would follow up and say I also did head counts and bed checks. My hours were long trying to pay the bills and keep food on the table, being a single parent. I still needed to protect her and keep her safe and make sure she was doing the right thing because I wasn't at home. So, I had to have strict rules.

Family holidays were nonexistent. The Thanksgiving holiday

was the best in the Ridgeway Family and I missed a lot of them. I made sure that Angela was there front and center. When I transferred out of Lexington my family made sure she was there. Someone would always make sure that I had plenty of pictures and phone calls. I cried every year. It got to the point that it became too much for me and I stopped calling home on Thanksgiving.

My marriage really suffered. It was so hard trying to hold a marriage together, working so many different shifts. I did stop working all those hours even though the different shifts were killing us. I remember having to work on New Year's Eve. He did all he could to pick me up before the count. He would have champagne already poured into the glasses for the New Year's toast. I made it but I was running. No matter how hard we tried, my career took a toll on the marriage. I had built the foundation of my career on that name. This was my second marriage. I found myself in a courtroom like the legendary Ms. Tina Turner fighting to keep his last name. I told the judge that was all I wanted because my career was built on that name. The judge granted my request and I was out. This sacrifice was more than I had planned. Maybe there are females out there who could have it all. I didn't.

Appendix

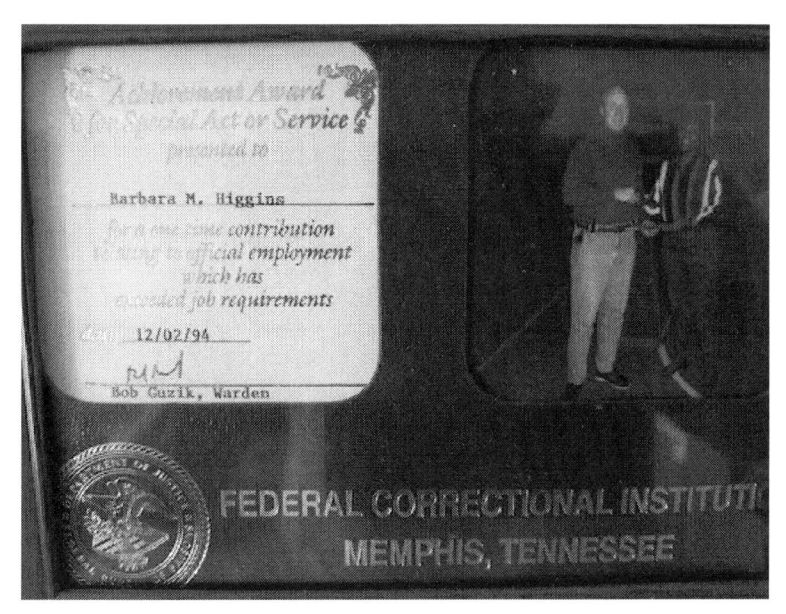

6) Achievement Award for Special Act Award
   FCI, Memphis, Tennessee

7) Achievement Award for Special Act Award
   FCI, Memphis, Tennessee

Into the Shadow

8) Quality Step Increase Outstanding Evaluation for the year
FCI, Memphis, Tennessee

9) Quality Step Increase Outstanding Evaluation for the year
FCI, Tallahassee, Florida

Appendix

10) Sustained Superior Performance Award
Tallahassee, Florida

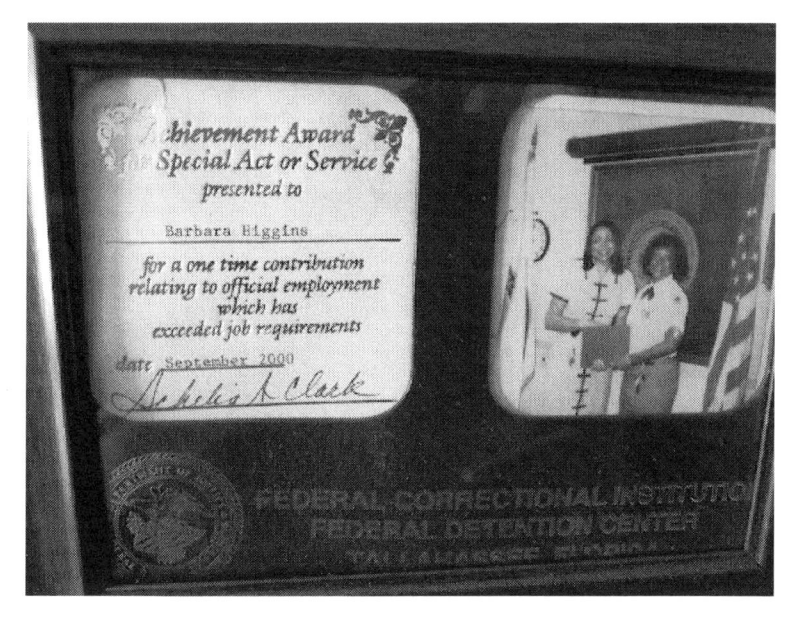

11) Achievement Award for Special Act
Tallahassee, Florida

12) Quality Step Increase Outstanding Evaluation for the year
Tallahassee, Florida

Appendix

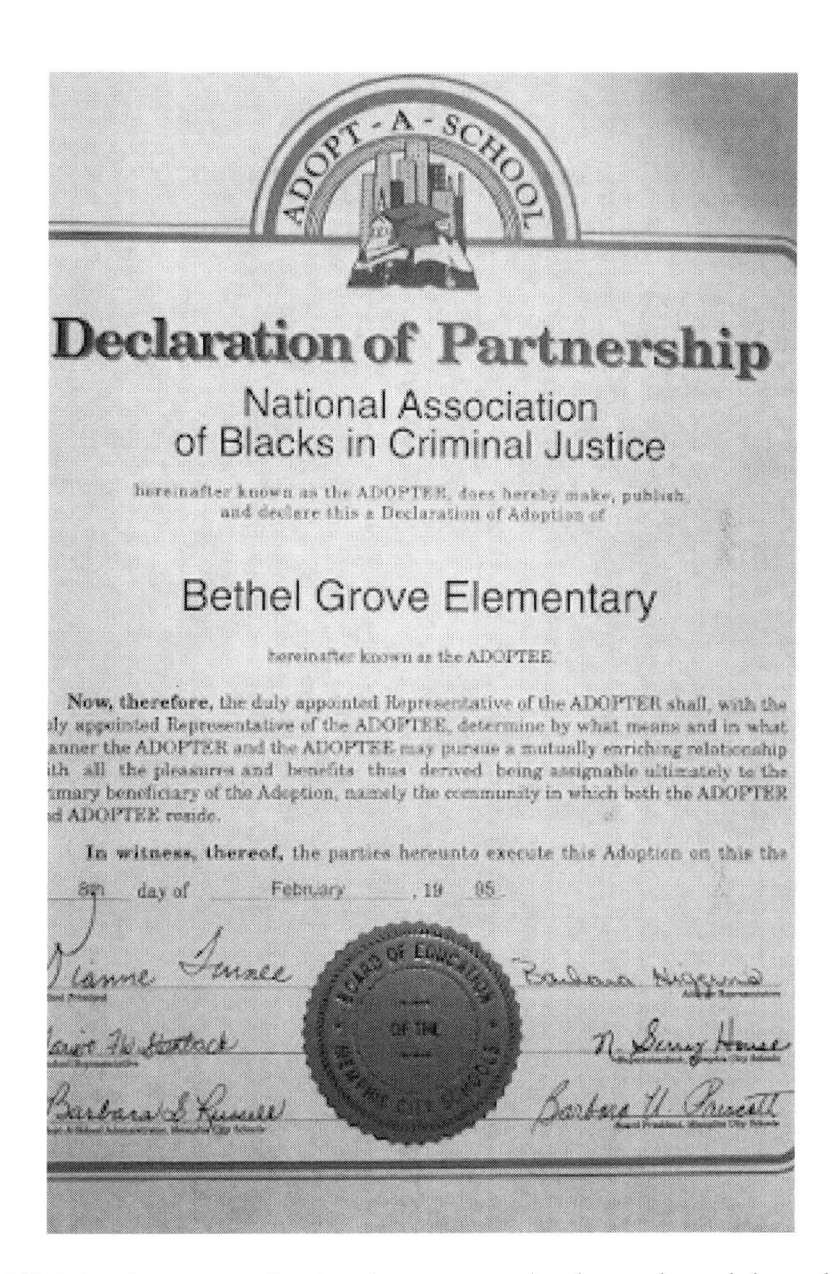

13) Adoption papers for the elementary school we adopted through the National Association of Blacks in Criminal Justice
Inter-City Memphis, Tennessee

Into the Shadow

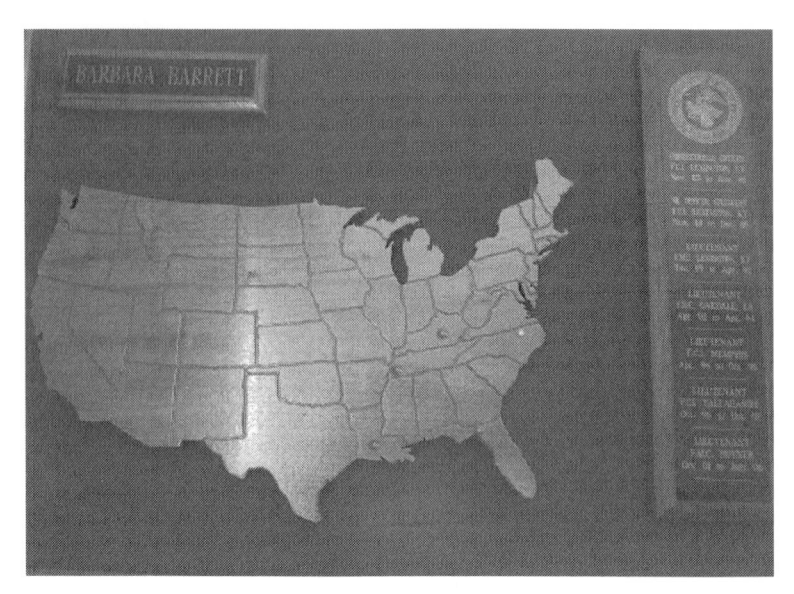

16) Map of the institutions I worked and reporting dates

17) Coach of the year!

Appendix

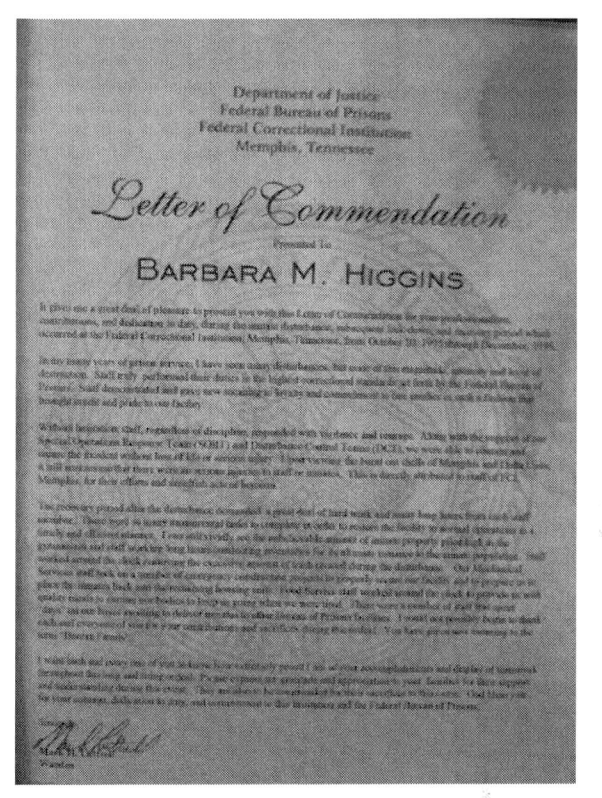

14) Letter of Commendation for the inmate disturbance
Memphis, Tennessee

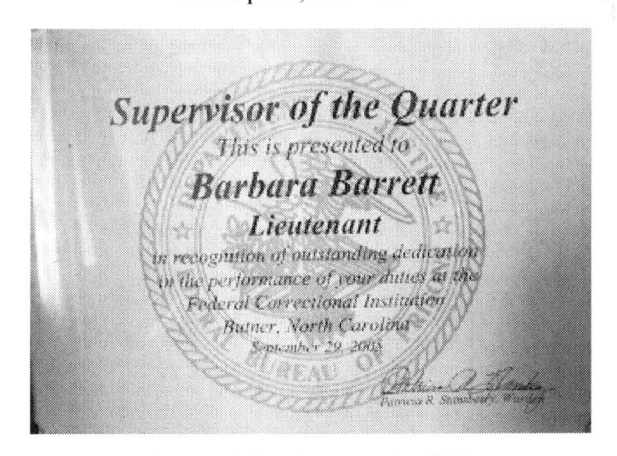

15) Supervisor of the Quarter in different name
FCI, Butner, North Carolina

17) My many faces

Appendix

18) Me today living my best life! Zip lining!

About the Author

    I am the seventh child of eight. Life in the Ridgeway family was a great one. My childhood was filled with love, life, and living. We left our front doors open, played in muddy ditches, and had to be home before the streetlights came on. There was an old schoolhouse yard that had been torn down and the field remained opened. That's where the magic happened. All the kids in the neighborhood would meet in the school yard to play tackle football (we didn't know anything about flag football at the time). There were many busted noses, as well as broken bones. We played baseball or softball, depending on what kind of ball we had at the time. But we didn't forget to be home before the streetlights came on. If I did, my mama would come and get me with a switch (small piece of a tree branch) in her hand and whip my butt all the way home, but to me it was worth it. I got my butt whipped often just to be a part of the magic on the school yard. On certain days I was not allowed to go past my aunt's house. The problem with that was the school yard was past my aunt's house. Me being me would go to the school yard and here would come Nellie Mae (my mom) with switch in hand. But on this particular day, I went back and whipped everybody who laughed. Life was good.

But then you grow up and think you're grown. I married my high school sweetheart who later became abusive in the marriage. He was a great boyfriend who took great care of me. Treated me like the queen I was raised to me. He would walk for an hour to my house if he didn't have a ride to visit me and then walk back if my father didn't take him home. Who wouldn't be impressed by that? We married and had a daughter, Angela. It took three years into the marriage before I could find my heart. It was one of those times where he had been out all weekend. I knew he was home before Monday because the one thing he did do was work and provide for me and Angela. On Saturday, instead waiting for this ass whipping, I strategized and placed items around the room to get my hands on. True to form. he came in and started on me. To his surprise I didn't back down. so when his hand struck, mine struck back. We were literally fighting like bitches in the street. At some point he knew he was losing control or power over me, so he pulled out a knife and started talking about what he was going to do to me. I was all in at this point, so I kept stepping back, never taking my eyes off of him. I knew that I had something in the corner I just had to keep moving backward. Finally my hand touched it, and I started singing hallelujah in my spirit. I had put hands on the wrought iron ashtray stand. You know the one with the gold cigarette tray. Yes, that one. I grabbed it and round housed his punk ass. That punk ass bitch was still laying on the floor when I left. I grabbed my daughter and never looked back. I was done. Like Maya Angelou's poem, **"And still I rise."**

I remember Tina Turner saying that you need an exit plan; that was mine. Like her I didn't have two pennies to rub together, but look at me now. I never in my life had backed down from anyone or anything and don't know why I did with him Never again in this life. Look at me now!

Made in the USA
Monee, IL
17 January 2020